Catechesis

An Invitation to Living Faith

Edited by Jarred Mercer

scm press

© the Editor and Contributors 2020

Published in 2020 by SCM Press
Editorial office
3rd Floor, Invicta House,
108–114 Golden Lane,
London EC1Y 0TG, UK
www.scmpress.co.uk

SCM Press is an imprint of Hymns Ancient & Modern Ltd
(a registered charity)

Hymns Ancient & Modern® is a registered trademark of
Hymns Ancient & Modern Ltd
13A Hellesdon Park Road, Norwich,
Norfolk NR6 5DR, UK

British Library Cataloguing in Publication data
A catalogue record for this book is available
from the British Library

978-0-334-05941-7

Typeset by Regent Typesetting
Printed and bound by
CPI Group (UK) Ltd

Contents

List of Contributors

Jarred Mercer, formerly a chaplain, postdoctoral researcher and member of the Faculty of Theology and Religion at Oxford University, is currently Rector of St Paul's Episcopal Church in Newburyport, Massachusetts, USA. He is the author of *Divine Perfection and Human Potentiality: The Trinitarian Anthropology of Hilary of Poitiers* (OUP, 2019) and co-author of *Love Makes No Sense: An Invitation to Christian Theology* (SCM Press, 2019).

Peter Groves is Vicar of St Mary Magdalen, Oxford and Senior Research Fellow in Theology at Worcester College, Oxford. He is the author of *Grace* (SCM Press, 2011), co-editor with John Barton of *The New Testament and the Church* (Bloomsbury, 2016), and co-author of *Love Makes No Sense: An Invitation to Christian Theology* (SCM Press, 2019).

Melanie Marshall is Associate Chaplain and Career Development Researcher at Merton College and former Chaplain at Lincoln College, Oxford University. She holds a DPhil in classics and is currently working on a combination of patristic and early modern projects.

Simon Cuff is Lecturer and Tutor in Theology at St Mellitus College, Honorary Associate Priest at St Cyprian's Clarence Gate, Coordinating Fellow of the Centre for Theology and Community, and on the editorial board of *Crucible*. His doctoral research was on the reception of Scripture within critical theory and his publications include *Only God Will Save Us:*

The Nature of God and the Christian Life (SCM Press, 2020) and *Love in Action: Catholic Social Teaching for Every Church* (SCM Press, 2019).

Jonathan Jong is Assistant Professor at the Centre for Trust, Peace and Social Relations, Coventry University.

Mark Clavier is Residentiary Canon of Brecon Cathedral and Chair of the Standing Doctrinal Commission for the Church in Wales. Formerly, acting Principal of St Michael's Theological College, Cardiff and Vice-Principal of St Stephen's House, Oxford, he is the author of a number of books on Augustine, consumerism, and delight, including *On Consumer Culture, Identity, the Church, and the Rhetorics of Delight* (Bloomsbury, 2018).

Clare Gardom is writing her doctoral thesis on Clement of Alexandria at Oxford University and is a catechist at St Mary Magdalen's Church, Oxford. She has taught in primary, secondary and university settings and has two young children.

Preface

Jesus leaves his disciples with a great commission in the final words of Matthew's Gospel:

> 'Go therefore and make disciples of all the nations, baptising them in the name of the Father and of the Son and the of the Holy Spirit, and teaching them to obey everything I have commanded you. And remember, I am with you always, to the end of the age.' (Matt. 28.19–20)

The commission is the source and fountainhead for the set of disciplines in the Church which together are called catechesis: accompanying enquirers and new believers to baptism and seeing them formed for a lifetime of Christian service and ministry.

In every generation and age of the Church, the Church has needed a renewal of these ministries. As patterns of culture and learning and communication change, so our means of formation change and adapt to the context. Attention to catechesis will always embrace deep listening to the people we are walking with, the unfolding of the Scriptures, encountering the living Christ in the sacraments and equipping God's people for a lifetime of everyday faith.

Renewal always happens in a return to our sources in Scripture and the great tradition of the Church, applied in fresh ways to our present context.

I am delighted to commend this deep dive into the tradition from a group of authors who are both theologians and practitioners in this deep discipline. May it be a rich blessing to you and enliven this vital part of your ministry.

+*Steven Oxford*

Introduction

JARRED MERCER

'Catechesis' comes from the Greek word for 'teaching', but it is more than just oral instruction or traditional education, it is a cultivation of a living faith within the community of the Church. Christian faith and theology are preformed in the sacramental, communal and missional life of the Church, and catechesis is an invitation into this lived reality. This book is an exploration into the nature of catechesis and how within our churches it can shape the Christian community into an instrument of renewal in the world through holistic formation. Each chapter affirms that the future of catechesis in the life of the Church is to be found in holistic discipleship; and the book explores this by examining catechesis in its relationship to Christian worship and liturgy, the teaching of doctrine, mission and social action, evangelism, preaching, communal life, the cultivation of virtue, and the sacraments.

The book can be divided into three main sections. Chapters 1 and 2 set the background for what follows by seeking to define the nature of the task of catechesis. Chapters 3 to 6 draw out the main foundations of the practice of catechesis seen in the opening two chapters: teaching theology, peaching, sacrament, and worship and prayer. Chapters 7, 8 and 9 then examine how catechesis shapes and forms our daily lives within and outside the church community through the cultivation of virtuous living, the formation of the Christian imagination, and the catechesis of children. There is no claim here to cover every aspect of catechesis, but rather to provide a foundation for those who seek to be involved in making disciples of Jesus

Christ by offering a framework in which to do so. Catechesis itself is the practice of shaping a new vision for one's life, aiding others to see the world as God sees the world. This book seeks to shape a renewed vision of that task itself, aiding those who guide others in faith to do so with confidence and joy.

Chapter 1 'Beginning Catechesis: Where Do We Start?' helps us to think about how we begin to move towards the aim of drawing others into a living faith. The chapter claims that catechesis begins as a school of prayer, in the study of Scripture, in the sacramental life of the Church (which is both the source and aim of catechesis), and in the life of the catechist, who models this life of learning through prayer, study of Scripture, and service. Chapter 2 'The Nature of Catechesis: An Invitation to Faithful Living' outlines the nature of catechesis – what it is and what it is not. Catechesis is an invitation to living faith because it is primarily an invitation to live in the way of Jesus. The word for catechesis contains within it the word for 'echo', and catechesis is centrally about learning to echo the life of Christ in the world today. Christ is the content of catechesis in that we are learning about Christ, but he is also the primary catechizer, leading us in the way we are meant to follow. This chapter presents catechesis as a way of living alongside Christ and calling others to do the same.

In Chapter 3 'Doing Doctrine: The Lived Experience of Christian Teaching' Peter Groves looks at the formal 'teaching' aspect of catechesis from a fresh angle. Christian teaching, or doctrine, is something that is done rather than thought. Catechesis welcomes people into this activity – into what is nothing less than the whole of the Christian life. This chapter uses a historical example of the rule of life of The Brotherhood of the Holy Trinity, a religious community in nineteenth-century Oxford, and the game of football to exemplify the nature of teaching doctrine as 'playing the game'. In the same way one learns football not just by studying rules or statistics on paper but by playing on the pitch, so one learns the Christian faith by living the Christian life.

Chapter 4 'Catechesis as Proclamation: Teaching the Faith through Preaching' shows how preaching is at the heart of catechesis. Melanie Marshall presents preaching as a 'story-telling' that not only tells a story but involves the hearer in the story. Good preaching brings the story of our salvation to bear on the hearer in a way that implicates us all in that story of Jesus. Preaching is also a direct catechetical act, not only because it involves instruction, but because the task of theology is actually taking place in the task of preaching. The preacher is engaging in the work of theology, as are the people, as they bring their life into dialogue with the text of Scripture and the narrative of Christ's salvation. Preaching informs, instructs and inspires, and all along it shows us how we need continual transformation and that none of us are finished with this journey of catechesis.

Chapter 5 'Sacramental Catechesis: Enacting Our Source and Aim' argues that while the sacramental life of the Church is the aim of catechesis – catechesis seeks to bring people to share in the sacraments – it is also its source. The whole life of the Church, including its teaching and instruction, flows from the grace of the sacraments. Catechesis is an invitation into this transformed life of grace and, because it is not only informational but transformational, it is itself inherently sacramental. As the sacraments are the location of Christian transformation, they make 'real' what we are attempting to teach. Human beings are sign and meaning makers, and the sacraments make sense of and give meaning to the fullness of Christian teaching.

Simon Cuff in Chapter 6 'Liturgy and Catechesis: Learning Christian Worship' uses a wide definition of liturgy as the habits and rituals of Christian communities in worship. He explores how liturgy itself is catechetical. It is as an aid that points beyond the particular priest, preacher or worship leader and towards Christ. The chapter explores how liturgy works as a safeguard against our tendency to proclaim ourselves inadvertently even when we attempt to proclaim Christ. The liturgy works as an important backstop against the inadvertent idolatry that Scripture consistently warns us against. The chapter also considers how liturgies can be celebrated to point more readily to Christ and offer a lively proclamation of the faith.

This nourishes a community not only in the act of worship itself but through a lifelong journey of living worship and learning faith.

In Chapter 7 'Catechesis and the Development of Virtue' Jonathan Jong speaks of catechesis in terms of the cultivation of virtue. Belief and practice, theology and ethics or morality are inseparable for Christians. The work of catechesis must therefore always be the work of character formation – what Christians, drawing on classical tradition, have long referred to as 'virtue'. Jong pulls on a long tradition of seeing virtuous living as both living in accordance with one's nature and virtuous living as *skilful* living. Cultivating virtue in catechesis means drawing people towards living more fully human lives in Christ and training people to live well, or skilfully, through the communal life and teaching of the Church.

Chapter 8 'Instruction, Delight and Persuasion: Catechesis as Rhetoric' claims that catechesis as presenting information or communicating core beliefs is useless without shaping the imagination that forms the framework for those beliefs. Mark Clavier shows us that catechesis does not happen in a social vacuum but rather in a world that uses our affections to shape how we perceive reality. People are convinced less through rational argumentation than through persuasive appeals to their affections, especially in a consumer culture awash with such persuasive appeals through advertising and the like. Catechesis is an inherently rhetorical process whereby people are (in the words of Cicero and Augustine of Hippo) 'instructed, delighted and persuaded' to imagine themselves and their world in new ways – that is, through the lens of the gospel rather than as controlled by the market. In that sense, catechesis should be seen not so much as a series of lessons but as a process of shaping the imagination and offering a new vision of the world and ourselves.

In Chapter 9 '"Let the Little Children Come to Me": Catechesis of Children' Clare Gardom picks up on earlier themes of the book, particularly those of imagination, affect, learning by doing, storytelling, and virtue development to explore how these are involved in the catechesis of children. As baptized children are full members of Christ's body, the catechesis of children is not separate from adult teaching and worship, but our approach to catechesis of children can in many ways be distinctive. The whole Church is responsible for bringing up young people to know that they are children of God. Gardom uses Clement of Alexandria's stylizing of Christ as *paidagogos* – a figure in classical education responsible not only for imparting information but for bringing children up in the right habits of mind and behaviour – to speak of how Christ is the model of how we teach the faith to children, and it is when children are enabled to find themselves in Christ's story that new disciples are made.

It should be obvious by now that this is not a book of catechetical material (our previous book *Love Makes No Sense*[1] might be of use for that purpose). Nor is it a history of catechesis or a discussion of catechetical methods. For this there are many and diverse useful materials available, including the excellent book edited by Bishop Steven Croft, *Rooted and Grounded*.[2] This book is rather a self-reflection and critique on the nature of catechesis itself, causing us to re-evaluate and think again about what it is we are doing when we seek to pass on our faith and why we are called to do so. I hope that whatever tradition, denomination or context you find yourself in, this book will be a valuable resource to serve you in the task of *traditio*, the 'handing on' of the faith we have received. It is a task of helping to form new ways of being in the world, the holistic transformation of people's lives, and it is a joyful pursuit of love and care. May you find encouragement for such a task in these pages.

Notes

1 Jennifer Strawbridge, Jarred Mercer and Peter Groves (eds), 2019, *Love Makes No Sense: An Invitation to Christian Theology*, London: SCM Press.

2 Steven Croft, 2019, *Rooted and Grounded: Faith, Formation and the Christian Tradition*, London: Canterbury Press.

I

Beginning Catechesis: Where Do We Start?

JARRED MERCER

Introduction

Christian catechesis began in the early Church as quite a rigorous process. The rigour involved in becoming Christian led Celsus (whom Origen wrote against) to write in about AD 180 that if all people wanted to become Christians, the Christians would no longer want them. Catechetical practice as reported and instructed by people such as Tertullian (155–240) and in the writings attributed to Hippolytus in the third century might lend Celsus's criticism some credence. Imagine three years of in-depth Bible teaching followed by intense fasting, pretty extreme personal interrogation, ritual bathing, daily exorcisms, and an all-night prayer vigil filled with further instruction and someone reading at you through the night leading up to your baptism at Easter.

All this following initial questioning about your life and profession upon your first visit to church, after which you would likely have to quit your job to become a catechumen in the first place. Just think how hard the 'church growth' moguls of our age would come down on you if you questioned every newcomer about the morality of their life and profession upon their first visit to church before letting them in the door! Second- and third-century catechesis went a few steps further than watching a video of a few priests or pastors discussing theology on a park bench or a church small group answering discussion questions at the back of a ten-page pamphlet on the creeds (not that there is anything wrong with videos and pamphlets!).

The strict separation from society required among the earliest Christians would later change, of course. Whereas for Tertullian one would not only have to change profession if, say, one was a soldier or actor, but also if one was a construction worker, stonemason or basket weaver (presumably because these skills might be used for the construction of and use in pagan temples), major cultural shifts in the fourth and fifth centuries would allow for a type of Christian living that is more 'in but not of' the world, to use a popular Christian trope. Catechesis then came to be a training up of a body of people who were in the world, living among and within the broader society rather than in more strict separation from it.

But there is a deep continuity here. In every case of properly Christian catechesis, the focus is on the formation of one's whole life – on transformation and not merely information. Catechesis is a cultivation of a lived faith within the community of the Church. Whether in the form of strict separatism in the second and third centuries, or holiness within society in the fourth and fifth, the aim and purpose of catechesis remain the same, and must remain the same for us.

The Aim and Purpose of Catechesis: Living Alongside Jesus

Christian faith and theology are a lived, practised and performed reality – performed in the sacramental, communal and missional life of the Church. And catechesis is an invitation into this lived reality.

In catechesis we are talking about the shaping of a certain and distinctive kind of life: the making of a certain and distinctive type of human being for a certain and distinctive community. It is a shaping of the Christian imagination, offering a new vision of the world, ourselves and of our God. This is not about merely disseminating the right information: memorizing creeds, the ten commandments, or theological formulae. Catechesis does depend on teaching, but the aim of that teaching is the holistic formation of people's lives because that is what the truths of our faith do. That is what theology is all about. The gospel does not inform us. The gospel makes us new creations.

And so all of our teaching, all of our thinking towards God, all theology is a lived, practised reality; because the purpose of orthodoxy, or right teaching, is not being orthodox. Having right belief, embracing truth, is important, but the purpose, aim and end of that orthodoxy is not being 'right', it is to live a life of outpouring love and mercy in the world, drawing all people to God in Jesus Christ, because the love of God has been 'poured into our hearts by the Holy Spirit, who has been given to us' (Rom. 5.5). The aim, the end, is to live alongside Jesus, or we might say, to live our lives in dialogue with Jesus' life.[1] This comes through teaching, yes, but teaching that is wedded to the grace of the sacraments and worship, the life of the community, service to the poor, evangelism of the lost, justice for the oppressed, hope for those in despair – it comes through the world looking more and more like the world Jesus shapes in his life, ministry, death and resurrection.

We don't want to think rightly about the Trinity, for example, in order to not think wrongly about the Trinity, in order to not be called heretics (those accused of not holding to right belief). That's not the point. We want to believe rightly about the Trinity because right belief is not having the right answer to a puzzle: 'how can 1+1+1=1?' Right doctrine of the Trinity has to do with finding ourselves in the midst of God's saving mission to restore all things to God's self, because the doctrine of the Trinity is not a puzzle at all, it's an invitation into the divine life: the life of the Father who sends the Son to us for our salvation, and the Spirit who draws all things back into the Father's love.

We do not want to think rightly about the incarnation – God's coming to us in the humanity of Jesus Christ – in order to score theological points or satisfy intellectual curiosity about how to best understand how Christ is both fully human and fully divine. We want to think rightly about the incarnation because it is where we meet God among us – from the humility of the manger to the agony of the cross, God among and within us, uniting us to one another and to God.

And so it goes for all doctrines. In Christian teaching, in doing theology we are not seeking right answers. Ultimately, we are seeking right or holy living in union with Christ through the Holy Spirit for the salvation of the whole world. Catechesis is simply inviting others to join us.

So the beginning of catechesis is ultimately the very life and mission of Jesus Christ. This is what we are after as we train up the Church – Christ's body – through the ministry of teaching, proclamation and catechesis.

So, if I am going to say something about 'beginning cat-echesis', I have to begin by stating the end of catechesis. We cannot know where or how to begin without the telos, the end or purpose, of the thing before us. We must be heading somewhere if we are to set off in the right direction. We have to have the end in sight, and the end is to bring people into communion with Jesus Christ in the life of the Trinity – sal-vation, redemption, new creation. In catechesis, that is our end – and nothing less than that is what is at stake.

Encounter and Evangelism

With that end in mind, it seems quite obvious that we begin by encountering the living God in the person of Jesus Christ. This means that beginning catechesis actually begins before beginning catechesis. We cannot truly begin catechesis without the shocking, unsettling trauma of encounter with Jesus Christ. Through the proclamation of the gospel, through our lives of service and mercy, and through the beauty of our worship and Christ's presence in the Eucharist and in the words of Scripture, we offer ourselves as a gift of Christ's love in the world so that people come into contact with Jesus, and this encounter is earth-shattering. The reforming of the imagination, the new vision of the world, is one resurrected from the trauma of the crucified Christ's encounter.

This is crucial because in catechesis we are not teaching about the Church and its beliefs. Catechists, preachers and teachers are not presenting an objective outsider's perspective. We are not putting on an interesting religion course. We are not talking about Christianity to show what 'it' is, but who we are. We are saying the Church lives, moves, thinks and believes in these ways, and you might like to live, move and believe along with her.

Believing God or believing in God is always first a matter of placing our trust in God.[2] We give ourselves over to God and spend our whole lives trying to figure out what it means to believe in God, or to discover more fully who this God is that we believe in. Our teaching and formation of others must reflect this. We are calling people to God, more than attempting to explain God. We are moving people by and towards the truth, more than proposing it.

Doctrine flowing from trust is indeed how we get good and true teaching, where our creeds come from, where what we have come to call orthodoxy was made. The doctrines of the Trinity, or of Christ, or of salvation, or of anything else, come from people loving and trusting God and working out what that means as a human community living before God in the world. The creeds are not abstract principles floating around in some ethereal truth sky, which we pluck out and write down so that everyone can check their ideas against them and make sure they haven't lost their way. All proper Christian teaching is the expression of the Church living with and before God, giving herself to God and being received and made new by God. There is no such thing as theology in the abstract.

Catechesis must first, then, be a calling: a call to renewal, to repentance, to devotion, to worship and prayer. It must be that new-fangled and trendy buzzword 'evangelism' (I always thought it was pretty basic, but some seem to speak of it as a shiny new thing!). If there is no encounter with the risen Christ, no trauma of meeting God among us, then catechesis doesn't make much sense, as it is about going deeper into that relationship with the triune God.

We have the perfect example of this at the beginning of the Church in Acts 2. Peter proclaims the gospel of Christ, crucified and risen, the people ask what they are to do, he tells them to repent and be baptized to receive forgiveness and the Holy Spirit. Verse 41 says 3,000 were added to their number that day. Verse 42 goes on to say that they 'devoted themselves to the teaching of the apostles and to the communal life, to the breaking of bread and to the prayers'. In other words, to catechesis. A winsome and persuasive presentation of the gospel of Jesus Christ, which captures hearts and transforms minds, must be at the beginning and bedrock of our catechesis.

It seems to me that we have lost confidence in our own story; indeed, what we would say is the story of everything. We are constantly looking to the world around us for reasons for our own existence, to justify a purpose for the Church, for effective ways to minister or present the gospel, because we have somehow lost confidence in our own identity as the people of the crucified and risen one. And because of this we have lost the ability to present our story with beauty, persuasiveness and winsomeness. We must begin by proclaiming: 'Here is the story, the heartbreakingly beautiful story of our Saviour who is God-among-us for our salvation, meeting us in the depths of our human life and struggle, and bringing every part of us into the warm embrace of God.' We must begin here, with evangelism towards encounter with Christ.

The School of Prayer

If the aim of catechesis is to become the people of the crucified and risen one, to encounter Christ and live alongside Jesus in his love and mercy in the world, then catechesis must also be and begin as a school of prayer. If we are to be renewed and shaped to share in God's mission in the world then both catechist and catechumens must live a life in God's presence through prayer. Catechesis might involve much more but it cannot be less than learning to pray.

Prayer is, first of all, simply acknowledging the truth that God is always present with and among us. To pray is to respond to God's presence and activity by living our own lives in God's presence and directing our own activity towards God. So if catechesis is about union with God in Christ and our own lives being shaped after God's action in Christ, then we must begin with prayer. God has given God's life to us in Jesus, and a life of prayer is a life given over to God in love and service – responding to God's gift by giving in return. In this sense prayer is a most basic action for living in the way of Jesus.

Learning the faith, learning Christian living, is learning through prayer. If catechesis is not going to be just about learning facts or propositions about faith, but a lived faith, an active life of progress towards the living God, then catechumens must be actively learning to pray. So as with evangelism and encounter, we must begin in the school of prayer.

Beginning with the Bible

Both these two aspects of beginning catechesis – proclaiming our story and learning to pray – necessarily mean that catechesis begins with the Bible. Scripture gives us a grammar to know God, to know how to speak about God, and how to speak back to God as it is the witness to Christ, God the Word. It also connects us with the full story and life of God's people, helping us to find ourselves in the midst of our 'family tree'.

When Augustine wrote to a deacon called Deogratias in the early fifth century, answering questions about instructing beginners in the faith, he as much instructs us today in our time. He tells Deogratias to teach the faith by rehearsing the narrative of God's love in the world, including the whole of Scripture and the history of the Church since the time of Scripture, directly claiming that this story is our story, too. And the aim of this historical account is that hearers would follow in that story of salvation – that they themselves would excel in living a life of love in Christ: 'Keeping [Christ's] love before you, then as a goal to which you direct all that you say', he instructs his pupil, 'recount every event in your historical exposition in such a way that your listener by hearing it may believe, by believing may hope, and by hoping may love.'[3]

Beyond Augustine, the example of the apostles in the Bible makes this biblical beginning of catechesis clear. We can look at Peter preaching his first sermon at Pentecost (Acts 2.14–41), Stephen giving his defence to the Pharisees (Acts 7.2–53), Paul speaking in the synagogue in Antioch of Pisidia (Acts 13.16–47), and so on, and see that the mystery of faith in Christ is explained through teaching the whole of the biblical narrative. The apostles learned this directly from Jesus himself, of course, who demonstrated the truth about himself from the law and the prophets (Luke 24.27), and claimed the authors of the Hebrew Bible wrote about him (John 5.46).

So as we begin with evangelism and encounter, and with the school of prayer, so we necessarily begin with Scripture.

Virtues and the Sacramental Life

The next point I want to make is that if the aim of catechesis is to encounter Christ and live alongside him, in continual transformation through our lives being in dialogue with the life and teachings of Christ, this means that catechesis, while having nothing to do with a modern moralist agenda, is about shaping virtuous lives – forming lives from which Christian virtues flow into the world; lives that show the produce, we might say, of the fruits of the Spirit. This is not just about right moral thinking or keeping rules. It's about the whole of one's life being shaped in a certain direction: the direction of the cross, the direction of the new creation – life that looks like Christ's life of self-giving love.

And this brings out the emphasis on the sacramental role of the Church's life in catechesis. If catechesis is about virtuous living, about living a life that looks like the life, death and resurrection of Christ, then we have to begin with the worshipping life of the Church. The grace that indwells us to live such lives flows through the waters of baptism and down from the altar, out of the doors of the church and into our streets through those who meet Christ at the font and at the altar.

While the sacrament is the summit of catechesis – we are bringing people to the point of meeting Christ in baptism or confirmation, or continually at the Lord's table – we cannot forget that the sacrament is also the source of catechesis, and the Christian life as a whole. This is the case naturally because of the grace that comes to us through the sacrament, but also because the sacrament and the liturgy supporting it have a didactic role in themselves. They teach us who Christ is and what it means to be Christ-like.

Take the example of small children. From the time they are newborns, we read to them, talk to them, sing to them, and they cannot comprehend a single word of what is being said. Why do we do this? Well, all of a sudden, often at around two years old, children start spouting out sentences. And it becomes clear that all along, even though they might not have been able to comprehend anything at all early on, their minds have been shaped, the language was taking root and they were growing up into that language and comprehension of it. Their formation was continually taking place.

The worship of the Church works similarly as it gives us a grammar for faith and teaches us the language of the faith. It is catechetical in that going through the motions of our worship opens us up to comprehension of the faith in new and deeper ways. People who are new to the liturgy may not understand everything that is going on, but they are being shaped and moulded more in the way of Christ through their act of worship – even when they don't realize it (like the infant learning language). And this means that we must lead and participate in the Church's liturgy with unabashed confidence. Many people seem to think that the fullness of Christian worship is something to be shy about, or that there may be children or people who are visiting or new to the Church and not yet ready for it. On the contrary, the liturgical, worshipping life of the Church is for them as much as it is for the seasoned Christian, and it works to reform our relationship to God, one another and the world. As we will see in Chapter 6, our worship and manner of worship shows to others what we believe about Christ – who we claim Christ to be and what we believe it means to follow him – and it is in that sense inherently catechetical, and for this, if for no other reason, we had better care deeply about what our worship is proclaiming.

Thus, as with evangelism and encounter, prayer and the Scriptures, we must begin at the sacramental and worshipping heart of the Church's life and mission.

The Life of the Catechist

I want to point out one more thing we find at the beginning and foundation of catechesis. If catechesis is about union with the triune God through Christ, and if catechesis is a school of prayer shaped by the Scriptures and the sacramental life that manifests Christ's self-giving love in the world through the Church, then catechists themselves need to be on that road of learning Christian living through prayer, study, worship and self-gift themselves. This involves not only devotion to worship and prayer, but also to theological learning. We should have a storeroom, a well of theology, being filled up by immersion in Scripture and the work of great theologians from which we continually draw.

If we are ordained, we have promised ourselves to this. In my tradition of Anglicanism, the ordering of deacons and priests requires the one being ordained to make a vow to a life of study and teaching, particularly of the Scriptures, and we are given a Bible (other traditions are often similar). In fact, in the ordering of priests in the Book of Common Prayer, five of the eight promises made by the person being ordained are centred upon study, teaching and formation of the life of the flock, whom it calls 'the great treasure', committed to the priest's charge. This is a clear calling from the pages of the Bible itself: We are to 'study to show [ourselves] approved unto God, [workers] that need not be ashamed, rightly dividing the word of truth' (2 Tim. 2.15).

The anti-intellectualism of our society has greatly influenced the Church, so that it seems priests and pastors are at times actively encouraged to forsake their vow of holy learning. I've heard numerous stories of ordained people being turned down for positions in churches or refused promotion for being 'too clever', or intellectual, or knowing too much theology, as people make the unverifiable and misguided assumption that such people are too lofty, care more about academic learning than pastoral care, or will be unable to communicate on a level others can understand.

I think this has a great influence on what I mentioned earlier about a lack of confidence in our own story, a lack of confidence in the gospel. This is something we must resist and overcome if we are going to begin and continue catechesis in a way that honours our Christian heritage, honours our life as ministers of the gospel for those of us who are ordained, and honours the people entrusted to us for their growth in holiness. We must begin with ourselves and our own unwavering devotion to prayer and study.

If the life of the catechist, though imperfect, is not driven in the direction of prayer, contemplation, love, generosity, holiness and sound learning, they have already failed before they have begun. And so we must begin our catechesis with the catechist.

Where We Do Not Begin

A brief note about where we should not begin. I hope it is clear by now that catechesis is not simply about acquiring right answers to 'God questions', that catechesis is not apologetics. If you look through much of contemporary catechetical material, the vast majority seems to begin with attempting to prove that God exists. This is very unfortunate, and it seems especially true of catechetical material aimed at young people. It is almost as if we are making an intentional effort to make people into bad theologians from as early an age as possible!

I hope I am not bursting your bubble when I say that the infinite, non-contingent, source and sustainer of all existence cannot be proven or disproven by finite beings, whose very existence is utter contingency and who can only use resources from a finite contingent world as tools for investigation. Richard Dawkins or other celebrity atheists may not demonstrate the philosophical or even logical acumen to figure this out, but I hope we do!

If you have ever picked up a catechetical resource and seen that the first lesson was entitled 'Proof of God's Existence' and you absolutely panicked, I hope that the idea that catechesis should not begin here puts you at ease. But it is also essential not to make catechesis about this sort of thing because we want in our catechesis to train good theologians; that is, train people up in that lived, practised reality – the performance of Christian doctrine. Beginning with false or even anti-theological categories that place God within the boundaries of material creation, as if God could be examined under a microscope, is probably not a good start at shaping theological minds.

This doesn't mean we ignore questions related to God's existence or other things that typically fall into the category of 'apologetics' (or defending the faith). These questions are extremely important, and no doubt you will be faced with them at some point in your life if you have not already. We should think hard and well about them. It means, rather, that we should not fall into the trap that much of Christian catechesis has in our age, of treating theology like a method of scientific enquiry rather than a lived, practised, reality, as if the methods we use for the study of God were much the same as a botanist studying conifer trees. God is not known in this way, and we are not beginning catechesis well if we begin by thinking towards God wrongly right from the start.

Conclusion

However, beginning with evangelism and encounter, beginning in the school of prayer, beginning with Scripture, beginning in the sacramental and worshipping life of the Church, and beginning with the catechist's own life, we can begin to envision a life of catechesis in the Church that does not merely posit information and find answers to our curiosities, as important as our curiosity is, but one that moves people. One that moves people further towards the fullness of life in Christ – that moves people towards new creation. And one that perhaps moves us towards a catechesis that has the proper end in mind: that of union with the triune God through encountering Jesus Christ.

Throughout this book each of these aspects of the beginning of catechesis will be looked at more closely, as will other aspects of the nature and practice of passing on the faith. At every turn, this encounter remains both the source and the aim.

Notes

1 See Rowan Williams, 1982 [2014], *Resurrection: Interpreting the Easter Gospel*, London: Darton, Longman and Todd, p. 76.

2 See Rowan Williams, 2007, *Tokens of Trust: An Introduction to Christian Belief*, London: Canterbury Press.

3 Augustine of Hippo, *De catechizandis rudibus* 4.8; 2006, *Instructing Beginners in Faith*, Raymond Canning (trans.), Boniface Ramsey (ed.), New York: New York City Press, p. 21.

2

The Nature of Catechesis:
An Invitation to Faithful Living

JARRED MERCER

The Nature of Catechesis: Moving Towards the Life of the Trinity

When we think about the nature of catechesis, we think first about teaching. The word 'catechesis' comes from the Greek word for teaching or oral instruction. It is a passing on, a *traditio* (literally, a handing down) of the faith as the Church has received it, understands it and lives it. The 'living' part is essential. This is really at the heart of what we mean by catechesis, here is where we locate its nature. Because this is not a tradition, a passing on, like that of handing on a baton in a race. The faith is not a ready-to-go, neatly boxed-up package to hand on to the next in line. We pass on the faith, we catechize, by 'stepping lively',[1] as it's been said, and through relationships of mercy, forgiveness, justice and compassion, we bring the faith to life in the real world, making it a lived experience.

In Chapter 1 we saw that catechesis, from the earliest Christians to now, is about transformation of the whole person, not just teaching or learning the right stuff. This is the end of catechesis; and this end of catechesis helps us to learn more about its nature – what catechesis is. This chapter fleshes this out a little bit more.

At the heart of it, I want to say that Christian catechesis is not teaching people about Jesus, but bringing people into communion, into intimacy, with Jesus, who brings us to that ultimate aim of sharing in the life and joy of the Holy Trinity.[2] Augustine in his instructions on catechesis puts it this way: in Heaven, 'side by side with the angels we shall then enjoy by sight that Trinity in whose ways we now walk by faith ... [and] we are then no longer to shout out [our] profession of faith using noisy words but to drink in the reality in an act of the most pure and fervent contemplation in that place of silence'.[3] The ultimate goal of all this speaking and teaching and instructing is the purity of silence before God. We are training, educating, people towards the presence of God. Helping to show a path of life that ends in the freedom and peace of the endless and invincible love of the Trinity.

This is why Augustine even talks about how much the manner in which we teach matters. He interprets 2 Corinthians 9.7: 'God loves the cheerful giver', in light of the task of the teacher. The deacon Deogratias, who wrote to Augustine for advice on teaching newcomers to the faith, had become despondent and discouraged in teaching others. When he delivered long addresses about the same old thing he found that he was not just distasteful to his listeners but was exasperating himself with his lack of enthusiasm and eloquence![4] Augustine advises him to develop an 'attitude of cheerfulness' by proclaiming and living in Christ's love:

> Christ came before all else so that people might learn how much God loves them, and might learn this so that they would catch fire with love for him who first loved them, and so that they would also love their neighbour as he commanded and showed by his example, who made himself their neighbour by loving them when they were not close to him but were wandering far from him.[5]

All of Scripture 'speaks of Christ and calls to love',[6] so that in our exposition of the story of salvation this love directs and calls us: 'Keeping this love before you then as a goal to which you direct all that you say, recount every event in your historical exposition in such a way that your listener by hearing it may believe, by believing may hope, and by hoping may love.'[7] It is only in resting in this love that the despondency we can experience in teaching turns to joy, for 'fluent and cheerful words will then stream out from an abundance of love and be drunk in with pleasure. For it not so much I who say these words to you as it is love itself that says them to us all, the love that has been poured out in our hearts by the Holy Spirit who has been given to us' (Rom. 5.5).[8]

Basically, don't be a gloomy bore that everyone hates to listen to! Inspire with joy and heartfelt thanksgiving to God and a continual attitude of love and service, but not just out of duty or obligation, but also as an outpouring of God's love that renews us and renews the listener even as we speak. Share our story as Christ's people with winsomeness and beauty – and don't be afraid of serious theology – because the aim is not getting people to think like us or handing people answers to their doubts and questions, but to turn hearts towards the pure joy of the life and love of the triune God. This in no way means we put on a fake smile and pretend that everything is wonderful all of the time. It rather acknowledges that even in the midst of utter darkness and desolation we are not left in despair. Christian 'cheerfulness' is not frenzied exuberance or glee – it often shares intimate space with deep sorrow. It is rather a recognition of where we find true delight, and a movement towards that delight's divine source: to 'drink in the reality' of our true home.

But how and why, we might ask, is God the Trinity our true home and source? At the heart of the Christian faith is the knowledge that God is love (1 John 4.7). Not that God contains love or possesses love as some sort of appendage or secondary attribute, but all that God is, is love, and everything comes from God and returns to God in love. In other words, you and I and all the world around us exists – we have our very being – in, from and towards God's love. God doesn't need us. It is not as if God were lonely or lacked the ability to love – needing some object for affection – and so created the world out of some lack or need. God has eternally existed as love itself, without needs and lacking nothing. We exist not because we have to, not because we are necessary or filling up something that was once missing for God, but simply because God chose us; simply because God's perfect love overflowed beyond Godself, bringing into being what once was not. We are in our very essence the objects of God's infinite affection and love simply because God wants to love us into existence forever. To not live in love, therefore, is entirely contrary to our nature. So, in this sense, catechesis – training people up into this love – is an effort to shape us into our true nature, forming more fully human people.

It is a bit of a theological trend to speak of our following in God's love, our fellowship with the Trinity, as if the Trinity were a 'model' for us to mimic. Much literature in modern theology describes the Trinity as a social model for us: in politics, economics, family life, and so on. But this really misses the point in an important way and also breaks with theological tradition. The life of God – that life of love as Father, Son and Holy Spirit – is incomprehensible and indescribable. The infinite by definition cannot be defined, it cannot be circumscribed, cannot be encompassed by our minds. There is no model we can derive from an infinite being entirely beyond our understanding that in no way fits into our categories of knowledge. We are finite and God is infinite, and it's no use pretending we can model the life of something that is forever beyond our grasp.

This is why what we call 'revelation' is so important: God revealing who God is to us in a way that is appropriate and attainable in our finite, created world. We talk about revelation through God's action in the world, through Scripture, and most essentially in Jesus Christ, who is God among us: the life of God lived out in human terms – made sense of within our finite human life and understanding. So if we want to know what our home and source look like, what it looks like to live the love we were created for, we shouldn't try to form abstract models from what we assume the infinite life of God is like, we should look to Jesus – the infinite life of God as expressed in finite humanity, condescending to human ways of knowing and being. The nature and aim of catechesis: sharing in the life and joy of the Holy Trinity, and showing a path that lives towards that life and joy, is ultimately then a path to follow Christ. The aim is not to create some abstract model for our faith, which inevitably ends up being a projection of ourselves anyway, but to recognize the divine life and love already among us, in the concrete reality of everyday human life in Jesus Christ, and to shape our lives in that direction.

As discussed already, catechesis is by nature necessarily a holistic enterprise. We are not just teaching people to ace a theology exam, we are seeking to shape whole lives towards glory and love. And this life of glory and love is the life of Jesus, who is God among us for our salvation.

The word 'catechesis' not only means 'teaching', but is also where we get our word 'echo'. Catechesis is about echoing the grace, mercy and love of God in the world – about living lives that echo the life of Christ.

The 'Echo' of Jesus: Christ as Catechist and Content of Catechesis

God demonstrates this holistic catechesis of love perfectly, and in God's self-revelation in Jesus Christ we have the ideal model of catechesis. Jesus is the content of catechesis – catechists are teaching others to follow Jesus – but he is also the ultimate catechist. Being an echo requires us first to hear. The love of God reverberates in our lives through our attentive ear first leaning in to receive God's Word, to receive God revealed among us in Christ.

Both the content and the aim of our catechesis is the life and mission of Christ himself, who is the lived expression of the triune God in our world, in our humanity; who is the new creation lived among us. Again, through our teaching, preaching, proclamation and catechizing, we are after new creation – the renewal of whole lives in the gospel – towards the perfect life and love of the Trinity. In Jesus that is exactly what we get. Jesus, crucified and risen, is the new creation, Jesus is the gospel, Jesus is the perfect life and love of God lived out among and within us.

When we look at Jesus as catechist we see that not only in preaching or telling parables or direct and intentional instruction, but just in the entire living of his entire life he is training others, shaping and educating others into that life of love. And so our Christian life, including the bringing of others to share in that life through catechesis, is a life on offer and available to all. It is a life that brings healing and renewal, that yes, corrects, but also encourages, and ultimately a life that forgives. Christ offers our broken lives back to us reconciled – restored and re-created. Catechesis brings us into contact with others to offer forgiveness and reconciliation too, because this is simply what the Christian life is, and we are seeking nothing less than forming Christians.

Catechesis is holistic transformation; it is new creation, because the content and model is Jesus himself. As Christ is the catechizer – both the way we are to follow and the very content of the way – catechesis necessarily involves continual dying and rising. Jesus Christ is the crucified and risen one, and so this is the content and the way of catechesis. We are walking people through death into resurrection life. In other words, catechesis is continual conversion.

Inviting people into the way of Jesus is necessarily inviting them to death and resurrection, to conversion, to brokenness and healing. Christ's destiny, of glory and of the cross, is our destiny, and true catechesis can be nothing less than the way there.

This is the 'trauma' of meeting Christ spoken of in Chapter 1. It is devastating, destabilizing, turning the whole world as we know it on its head. Jesus challenges where we place our trust, where we put our hope, what we desire, what we think is 'success' or fulfilment. He also challenges what we think is possible, bringing about new possibilities for who we can be and become as his body in the world. All of our expectations, our entire vision of the world crumbles in meeting Jesus and is reborn as something that we never knew or expected, maybe we never before could expect.

We are called through our life of learning the way of Jesus to become a people that when the world comes into contact with us it is a traumatic experience, just as to come into contact with Christ himself is such an experience.

What I distinctively and emphatically do not mean by this is that we play the silly games of 'culture wars' and try to confront the world in a sanctimonious manoeuvre of violent idealist aggression. Unless you've been asleep for decades, you must know exactly what I mean. This is a very different sort of 'trauma' of so-called Christianity confronting the world. If you're the person always sitting around having conversations about how the western world is morally going to hell in a hand-cart and you are the poor, 'persecuted' Christian who is constantly offended by the world's evils, then not only are you not following the way of Jesus, the true catechist, but you're not even the kind of person Jesus would spend time with! Jesus liked those people who knew they were sinners in need of grace and acceptance and had no time for the sanctimonious Bible-toting bullies of the world. These people inflict a negative trauma – they injure and harm, rather than heal.

What I mean by saying the way of catechesis is becoming people for whom the world to meet is a point of 'trauma' is that our lives should subvert our consumerist, hyper-individualist, self-absorbed, narcissistic society to the point that people should come into contact with the Christian community and see the world flipped on its head, as it is when we meet Jesus. They should say, 'Here is where self-giving love fuels a community, not self-aggrandizement and self-promotion. Here is where communion is the heart and soul of a society, not discord and aggression. Here is where all find a home in welcome and embrace and in seeing this I can never see this divided world the same again.' That should be the world's experience of coming into contact with those who call themselves 'the body of Christ'.

Catechesis is conversion, dying and rising, because Christ is both catechist and the way of catechesis, and Christ simply is the crucified and risen one. In catechesis, we are guiding people towards the life that moves through death, towards the 'trauma' of meeting Christ. And this means that catechesis, as we saw in the previous chapter, is also evangelism. And this evangelism, this welcoming of others into this encounter with Christ, this embrace, is offered through the communal life of the Church (the 'trauma' would not be so revolutionary if it simply affirmed rather than confronted our society's incessant individualism). Catechesis is by nature ecclesial action.

Ecclesial Action: The Community of Catechesis

Gerard Baumbach speaks of the nature of catechesis as making 'at church' 'as Church'.[9] At church we are still, we have silence, we, for once, slow down and stop moving, and we listen (hopefully!). We are communal and not individualist, we eat together, we offer our lives to God and to others, we reflect, we orient our lives towards what matters, and we remember – we recall collectively our betrayal, our violence, our rejection of love. We are united by our victimizing of Christ and saved by Christ our victim. Catechesis is making this not the reality of an hour on Sunday morning ('at church'), a performative dramatic exercise, but the reality of our entire existence ('as Church'): a eucharistic community, a community of universal gift on offer for the life of the world. We are becoming, we are, the community of eucharistic gift, and in catechesis we are welcoming others into this community.

This again emphasizes that Christianity is not so much about thinking the right thoughts and opinions about things. It is more about where we abide. It is about belonging, about being the community of the crucified, and so catechesis is first and foremost inviting people in. It is through pain and suffering and joy walking through life together towards our ultimate end in the endless love of God. It is essentially and necessarily communal because it is about belonging to Christ's family, the Church, but it also needs to be communal for a very practical and pastoral reason.

If faith in Christ, becoming Christian or being catechized, is not simply verbal affirmation of belief or sound doctrine, but a movement of one's whole life through death and into new life – that trauma of confronting the living God in Christ – a movement from all that is safe and familiar into new territory fraught with risk, then everyone needs as much support from the community as possible. Simple as that. No one can go at this alone. Teaching someone the right things without them worshipping with the community and coming to share in our family meal at the altar, without them spending time with others and learning the way of Jesus by example and through living it alongside others, you might help shape people who can write a theological essay but you won't be making genuine followers or 'echoes' of Christ.

But if when they are sick or depressed or hurting or grieving you are with them, if when they are struggling with sin or fear or loneliness the community is with them, if when they doubt or struggle you are there saying, 'so do I'; if when the needs of the poor around you are met by you and the catechumen is there with you seeking to bring new life to others, or if the catechumen is in poverty themselves the community does all they can to bring them out of it (whether or not they ever convert or think the right things); if you don't just offer a course for people to learn orthodox doctrine (good though that is), but welcome those who feel lost or rejected or cast out and show them that God loves them and that you love them; then you will be making Christians, a community of universal gift, of self-giving love – then we will hear echoes of Christ in the world. After all, 'there is nothing that invites another's love more than to take the initiative in loving'.[10]

Augustine can therefore write so movingly that the gift given to both the catechist and the catechized is 'to taste [true rest's] sweetness and delight even here amid the most bitter troubles of this life'.[11]

Through the proclamation of the gospel, through our lives of service and mercy, and through the beauty of the liturgy and Christ's presence in the Eucharist, we place ourselves on offer as a gift of Christ's love in the world so that people come into contact with Jesus, and this encounter must be a holistic reformation of lives; a formation of real people into living echoes of Jesus Christ – lives that are in constant dialogue with Christ's life, constantly bucking up against perfect love and discovering aspects of ourselves that need renewing in the way of that love.

As seen in Chapter 1, catechesis is holistic, it is conversion, it is evangelism, it is ecclesial invitation. And it is these things because it is essentially and fundamentally an invitation to communion with Jesus, that we might become the eucharistic community of self-gift on offer for the world; the 'echo' of Christ's self-giving love.

Notes

1 Gerard F. Baumbach, 2017, *The Way of Catechesis: Exploring Our History, Renewing our Ministry*, Notre Dame, Indiana: Ave Maria Press, p. 5.

2 See John Paul II, Apostolic Exhortation, 1994, *Catechesi Tradendae (On Catechesis in Our Time)*, Catholic Truth Society, 5; referenced in Baumbach, 2017, p. 3.

3 Augustine of Hippo, 2006, *De catechizandis rudibus* 25.47, *Instructing Beginners in Faith*, Raymond Canning (trans.), Boniface Ramsey (ed.), New York: New York City Press, p. 104. See the excellent introduction in this edition by Canning for the structure of Augustine's work and a summary of Augustine as catechist.

4 *De catechizandis rudibus* 1.1, 2006, p. 4.

5 *De catechizandis rudibus* 4.8, 2006, p. 19.

6 *De catechizandis rudibus* 4.8, 2006, pp. 19–20.

7 *De catechizandis rudibus* 4.8, 2006, p. 21.

8 *De catechizandis rudibus* 14.22, 2006, p. 55.

9 Baumbach, 2017, p. 9.

10 *De catechizandis rudibus* 4.7, 2006, p. 17.

11 *De catechizandis rudibus* 16.25, 2007, p. 67.

3

Doing Doctrine:
The Lived Experience of
Christian Teaching

PETER GROVES

Any theology of catechesis must be practical. One of the greatest of Christian teachers, Thomas Aquinas often invoked Aristotle to remind his readers that teaching is only teaching if learning is taking place. One can stand in front of an audience and lecture until one is blue in the face, or one can engage in the most detailed explanation of a difficult problem to a single conversation partner, but if neither the audience nor the tutee is paying any attention, then one is not teaching, one is simply talking. Teaching is, then, what the British philosopher Gilbert Ryle calls an 'achievement verb'. It is defined not by the agency of the person trying to teach, but by the receptivity of the person who is learning.

The teaching of the Christian faith is no different. Catechesis that does not enable learning is not simply inadequate, it is not catechesis at all. The practice of Christian teaching is always rooted in the practicalities of the context and the community in which that teaching is taking place. The particular context I intend to explore in what follows is the Church of England. That does not, I hope, restrict what I have to say to Anglicanism, but there are reasons why Anglicanism is a convenient context from which to explore catechesis, and they are largely to do with what some see as its major weakness: lack of definition. The inability to express, in a series of propositions, the essence of Anglicanism is akin, one might suggest, to the impossibility of reducing Christian doctrine to propositions alone. Such a reduction can't be achieved not because of any theological inabilities on our part (though theology that is unaware of its limitations is hardly worthy of the name), but because of the nature of Christian faith and teaching, which is always practical and, despite the efforts of theologians, never something abstract.

The Austrian philosopher Ludwig Wittgenstein had much to say about following rules, and his interpreters have had much to say about what he meant by it. Those debates don't prevent us from learning that, for Wittgenstein, rule-following serves as one among several important concepts under which we can examine and understand the practicality of language and meaning. The philosopher, if not misguided, will attend to the use of words in their contexts, to the language games that make up our communication, with the forms of life that characterize human function and interaction. The solipsist, trapped within his thought experiments, is in fact dependent upon the world around him to construct his misguided philosophical imaginings. Words and concepts take their meaning from practice.

Theologians, late to the party as so often, have caught up with Wittgenstein in the last half century, most famously through the work of the late great Yale professor George Lindbeck and his respondents.[1] The word 'doctrine' simply means teaching, and teaching is an activity, an activity that depends on learning. So doctrine – teaching – is something the Church does. It is not a set of abstract propositions to which we make intellectual assent. Rather, it is the grammar of Christian life and practice which we perform in every aspect of the Church's existence. If this is the case, it will follow that catechesis is not primarily about learning atoms of information, still less acquiring a large number of theological facts. (Theologians influenced by Wittgenstein might well deny that there can ever be theological facts, but such a view is rather unfashionable these days.)

Theological vocabulary is important here. Catechesis is the practical engagement with Christian discipleship in which the Church and its members are all always involved, since to be a disciple is to be one who learns. The specific place of catechesis within the Church's teaching ministry, in feeding and encouraging new and growing Christians, is always something that takes place within the practical context of the Church's life, and is not an addition or an alternative to that practical Christian living.

A Catholic Anglican Perspective

Within the swirling theological perspectives of Anglicanism, many subdivisions may be encountered. The Anglican identity from which these reflections emerge is a catholic one, that is to say, one that takes inspiration from the breadth of catholic and sacramental theology throughout Christian history, and which owes a particular debt to the theologians and teachers of the nineteenth century who sought to reassert that sacramental identity for the Church of England in what we now call the Oxford Movement. Writing from this catholic Anglican perspective, I hope what follows will chime with readers of all traditions and denominations, concerned as we are to learn the practice of Christian teaching together. Catholic Anglicanism's gifts to the wider task of Christian theology are many but very important among them is the gift of being wrong. As we shall see, an evidential or fact-based account of Anglo-Catholic theology can no longer carry the day – we have learned too much about history and theology since those Victorian debates were in full flow. But the reality of catholic Anglicanism remains, and it remains first and foremost because it is practised.

For reasons rather different from those of Wittgenstein, Anglo-Catholics were rather keen on the following of rules. The Oxford Movement, the aforementioned attempt to recapture the Church of England's catholic and sacramental life (and sometimes called Tractarianism after its theological tracts published to that end), began in England in the 1830s. Not long after its inception, a revival of interest in the religious life within the Church of England led to the foundation of sisterhoods and brotherhoods living together under a common Christian rule. Edward Pusey was a major figure in this process. At the same time, devotional societies, tangentially connected with this monastic revival, sprang up and among them was one in Oxford which called itself the Brotherhood of the Holy Trinity. Originally called the Brotherhood of Saint Mary it was founded in Advent 1844 as a society dedicated to the appreciation of ecclesiastical art, but it quickly changed into a devotional brotherhood, and was formally refounded as such in 1852. It was largely a society of students, and its members, or 'brethren', included several young men who would become highly significant in the Victorian Church, among them Henry Parry Liddon, Edward King, William Bright, Richard Benson and Alexander Forbes, already by this time Bishop of Brechin. The organization remains largely forgotten, but was significant for many of those who are important to the development of what was becoming Anglo-Catholicism. Scholarly attention to the group has generally centred on Gerard Manley Hopkins who, as an undergraduate at Balliol College, was connected with the Brotherhood through several close friends, including Robert Bridges and Vincent Stuckey Coles. Hopkins adopted many of the Brotherhood's practices, despite in the end deciding against formal membership, and his early poem, 'The habit of perfection', which concerns the disciplines of self-denial, was composed at the time of these close associations.

The Brotherhood's rule was founded upon seven objectives:

1 To rise early.
2 To be moderate in food.
3 To devote some time in each day to serious reading.
4 To speak evil of no man.
5 To avoid dissipation.
6 To commemorate the Holy Trinity, by saying the Gloria Patri on first rising and the last thing at night.
7 To pray for i) the unity of the Church, ii) the conversion of sinners, iii) the advancement of the faithful, and iv) the members of the brotherhood generally.[2]

Added to these objectives, however, were 15 'rules to be aimed at', which testify to the earnest if somewhat precious piety of these high-church young men. They include the exhortations 'to shun all unedifying and frivolous conversation, especially when in female company'; 'When in society, not to eat above three kinds of food, besides soup or fish'; 'to avoid attendance at the theatre and opera, as well as all places and practices in any way connected with the promotion of known sin'; and 'to keep careful guard over the eyes, when in the streets or elsewhere, so as not to look at anything hurtful unless it is a duty'.[3]

These 'rules to be aimed at' would raise an eyebrow or two today. But they were a central part of the life of these young men. Examining the proceedings of the Brotherhood's meetings, one quickly discovers a recurrent controversy. It concerned the rule, and always centred on the same question. Could or should the 'rules to be aimed at' be made obligatory? In 1857 a stricter observance of the rule was advocated. It was suggested that brethren who wished to could take on the 'rules to be aimed at' as obligatory for a Lenten discipline. In 1862 Luke Rivington, later of the Society of Saint John the Evangelist (the 'Cowley Fathers'), raised questions in a chapter meeting about the status of the 'rules to be aimed at'. No changes were made. The question resurfaced in 1864, as to the character of the obligation the 'rules'. The Minute Books record:

> The Master answered – 'They were not strict rules, but rules strictly to be aimed at, plainly not to be forgotten. The phrase was used to draw a limit between absolute Rules, which might be a snare, and if broken, must be confessed as a sin, and on the other hand mere lax rules, which might be looked on only as suggestions. The rules were to be kept prominently before the mind, and resolutely aimed at as far as possible.[4]

In 1865 the argument concerning the rules was repeated far more vehemently, with William Bright and Richard Meux Benson, by then the Master, disagreeing fiercely. A new set of the Brotherhood's manuals was to be printed, and several members saw an opportunity to make the 'rules to be aimed at' obligatory. A series of debates followed, concerning which Bright wrote to Liddon at length on 7 June 1865, urging him to dissuade Benson. Vincent Stucky Coles, in a memoir of Liddon written for the latter's biographer, recalls that 'there were stormy times in the B.H.T. when violent differences arose as to the way in which the Rule was to be interpreted, but Liddon was not much concerned in these. He held aloof from the meetings, as at a later time he avoided the council meetings of the E(nglish) C(hurch) U(nion) and did his part by letters and private advice.'[5]

Bright and others suggested that, rather than making the rules obligatory, the Brotherhood should increase in number the seven original resolutions, avoiding the stringency that some were advocating. Benson disputed the competence of the chapter meeting to discuss this, and a committee was appointed to report back in a year. The argument faded away when it did, and its proposals were defeated at the chapter meeting of 30 May 1866.

Thinking and Doing

Why spend our time considering what seem to be a series of petty disagreements on the part of university students who might have benefited from a little more fun in their lives? Their example is useful for a number of reasons, but chiefly because of the ways in which we see them responding to the Christian call to holiness and discipleship. Here we have a group of young men, zealous for Christ and the gospel, whose imaginations have been thoroughly captured by the revolution of the Oxford Movement. They see the Church changing before their eyes, and they want to be a part of it. Thinking and arguing is all very well, and the deliberately controversialist nature of Tractarianism should not be downplayed. But the Brotherhood's passionate response dates from the 1860s, from the time of the ritualist controversies and the increasingly aggressive confidence of a new form of Anglicanism engaged in mission far beyond Oxford. It is no accident that the brethren record sending messages of support to clergy such as Charles Lowder in London and Arthur Wagner in Brighton. Lowder was at the heart of the passionate and even violent disputes concerning the introduction of catholic liturgical practices to Anglican worship in London's East End; Wagner had been legally condemned and publicly pilloried for refusing to comment upon the content of a sacramental confession made to him by a young woman accused of murder. These two priests were, for the young men of the Brotherhood, contemporary martyrs for the faith. The students, by their membership of the society and the devotional habits that they practised, were engaged in their own personal ritualism, their shared contribution to what they saw as the struggle. The issue that was most important to them was the rule, the practical, prescriptive content of the common life to which they had signed up. Chief among their concerns was not so much what they thought as what they did. The practice of the faith was all important.

One might recognize in these young men the youthful zeal which has never left catholic Anglicanism. If there is self-knowledge in any passionate Christian practice, it must include an awareness of the limits such passion can place upon any particular theological perspective. Anglo-Catholicism, like many other Christian parties, has always had to confront its own theological immaturity, a childish tendency to see virtue in extremism, and to encourage a sectarian interest in being 'sound'. These tendencies are nothing new – the squabbles of different theological groupings are as old as the New Testament. Tribalism takes different forms in different contexts. Fortunately for its adherents, Anglo-Catholicism showed a remarkable propensity for change and development, right from the beginning. Even among the precious young men of Victorian Oxford one can see the foundations for growth which would enable Christian maturity, and those foundations are entirely practical. It is by doing, by practice, that that growth is made possible.

More importantly, however, and more pertinently for a reflection on the task of Christian learning, there is a great deal to be learned from just how wrong those early Anglo-Catholics were. So extraordinarily successful was the rhetorical aggression of the Oxford Movement that generations of Anglicans were already beginning to accept without question the Tractarian account of the Church's history. John Henry Newman's Tract 90 is only the most famous example of a series of tours de force in which one high-church theologian after another argued powerfully and persuasively that black was white. So the Church of England was never Protestant in its theological character, the Book of Common Prayer was a thoroughly Catholic document, luminaries such as Thomas Cranmer and Richard Hooker didn't really say what it seemed that they were saying in their theological writings, and certainly should not be called Protestants. The Thirty-nine Articles were not problematic for catholic theology, Anglicans had always believed in the real and objective presence of Christ in the Eucharist and so on and so forth. All evidences of Anglican Calvinism were aberrations, the Church of England was always Catholic with a large C and reformed with a small r, and you just had to apply the appropriate lens of interpretation to understand its history correctly.

That was the historical manifesto of the catholic revival in Anglicanism. It is to that historical understanding that millions of Anglicans owe their present existence and identity. And that understanding is most interesting because of the fact that it is pretty much altogether wrong. One could pick apart the details point by point with the aid of any well-informed history book. Anglicans and others have come to recognize that no academic historian takes seriously the notion that the sixteenth-century Church of England was not Protestant. Pointing to oddities such as the non-appearance of the word 'Protestant' in the Prayer Book will offer little defence against the overwhelming consensus of scholarship, not to mention the historical evidence itself. The Tractarians were historical revolutionaries and they stood history on its head, very effectively. But most things that are stood on their heads are in need of being righted.

Of course there is exaggeration in the way I have presented the errors of my own ecclesial identity. Of course there are also essentials I have omitted, not least the providential continuity of apostolic succession. But the important remains: the intellectual, propositional account of catholic Anglicanism which the Tractarians argued has been eclipsed. The practice of Anglo-Catholicism has not. Those earnest young men of the Brotherhood of the Holy Trinity remain our brethren not because of what they argued, but because of what they did. That which we uphold of their doctrine – the catholic theology of the Church and the sacraments – flowed from something they did – prayer, worship, liturgy – not something they thought. Intellectual claims alone did not hold muster. Following a rule gave them something to do which shaped their catholic theology.

Catechesis is always about doing. If we manage nothing more than imparting some propositional claims, and inviting others to remember them and pass them on, we are not doing very much doctrine, because we are not imparting Christian learning and, as was noted at the outset, if people are not learning then we cannot be teaching.

Playing the Game

When talking about rules, we had recourse to the ideas of Ludwig Wittgenstein. Another aspect of this thought, which has found its way into all sorts of contexts far removed from philosophy, is his appeal to the playing of games as an analogue for practice and hence, for him, an analogue for meaning and understanding. It is also, we might suggest, a very helpful analogy for the practice of Christian doctrine.[6] The world's most popular participation sport is usually all over our screens and news media. Its absence owing to the coronavirus pandemic was mourned by very many. The popularity of football is closely connected with its simplicity – you only need a ball and some players. However, to make a game work, people must have some ideas in common. We call this knowing the rules of football, and by those rules we don't mean the official laws of the game so much as the basic idea of using one's feet not one's hands, and trying to kick the ball into a goal. There are official laws that arbitrate at formal levels of participation, but it would be highly unreasonable to claim that a kick-about in a children's park was not a game of football. We know what is and is not a game of football because we know how to play that game.

Doctrine – the practice of the Christian life – is in this stretched analogy the game of football. It has lots of different aspects. Tactics, shirt colours, physical fitness, psychology and skill are a few. We could find ecclesial parallels in activities such as liturgy, preaching, prayer, fellowship, pastoral care and evangelism. We could differentiate the overall task of playing the game from the tweaks and definitions we need to make the game work. The former is doctrine, and is all embracing. The latter is what theologians call dogma – those precise definitions that the game requires in order to make it work. The lack of a universal precision applicable in every context does not matter: at a serious or professional level, the pitch on which the game of football is being played will be delineated out by white paint. In a social game, the pitch may be agreed by those coming together to play. Either way, the existence of a pitch is a common assumption, as is the position of the goals, whether marked by jumpers or goalposts. Dogmatic and credal definitions might mark out the lines or prescribe the rules for scoring a goal, but far more significant for the act of learning to play the game is the simple act of playing the game. Doing doctrine is then doing what the Church does.

Christian doctrine is a particular activity, playing this game and not another one. If I'm playing in a park and run off with the ball to a space three pitches away, I might still be playing, but I'm not playing that game. If I pick up the ball and run with it, I am no longer playing football (or at least, not 'association football'). Likewise, if I suggest that a sensible ecclesial course of action is the abandonment of the doctrine of the Trinity, then I am no longer playing this game, no longer practising Christian doctrine. I have abandoned the rules to which all have tacitly agreed by playing the game.

An obvious difficulty presents itself. Does this mean that there is no fluidity to the task of doctrine? Is Christian faith static? What of perhaps the most famous theological outpouring of the Oxford Movement, the thinking of John Henry Newman on the nature and development of doctrine?

We meet this difficulty by acknowledging that the rules do change. They change as the game develops, as all historians of sport know. According to invented tradition, an individual schoolboy did pick up a football and run with it, and in so doing made up a new game, the game we now call rugby. But we can also respond by forcing our footballing metaphor into just one more contortion and give some consideration to training and tactics and the way the game of football works.

It is a characteristic of modern professional football that standards of defending have improved out of all recognition in the last couple of generations. Teams are painstakingly coached to adopt and to keep to a playing shape as a group, with all ten outfield players moving in response to one another to hold that shape and keep it tight, as the saying goes. The more organized is a team's shape, the less likely is that team to concede a goal. However, it is of course difficult for a team to move forwards swiftly as one. If rapid progress is required, a much more likely scenario is that one player will burst forward, and the rest of the team will follow, adjusting their positions quickly to catch up with the forward player and reform their playing shape much higher on the pitch.

How do we know, then, whether to adjust the shape of the team? How do we decide whether to follow the player who has broken forward? The answer, of course, is – does that player have the ball? If she does, or a teammate close by has the ball, then the team as a whole will move to connect with them. If the ball is elsewhere, we will either lament that player's reckless charge forward and instruct them in defensive discipline, or commiserate with them on being tackled and encourage them to have another go at the first possible opportunity.

Either way, we learn from the effectiveness of the sally forward. We learn if we get it right, and we learn if we get it wrong. The Oxford Movement was a sallying forth, a bold and imaginative striking out on the part of some visionary doers and thinkers. But it was the doing, the practice of the catholic faith, which has lasted. Had we been left only with the Tractarian reading of history, we would now be staring at an empty nest. We would have charged forward, only to discover that we had lost control of the ball and the rest of our team was now thoroughly out of position and entirely vulnerable to a lightning counter attack by the Manchester City or Liverpool of Anglicanism, whoever that may be. As it is, the emphasis on doing, on following the rules, on playing the game, has kept us focused on the purpose of the game – God – and we can set about progressing through the tournament.

If playing the game is what we seek to do, then learning the game will be of the utmost importance. The point hardly needs making: one does not learn to play football by studying the laws or by reading the published documents of the Football Association. One learns by playing the game. Catechesis – doctrine – is about doing.

Notes

1 George Lindbeck, 1984, *The Nature of Doctrine: Religion and Theology in a Postliberal Age*, Philadelphia: Westminster Press.

2 *Brotherhood of the Holy Trinity Minute Book 1*, 1852, Pusey House, Oxford.

3 *Brotherhood of the Holy Trinity Manual*, 1858, Pusey House, Oxford.

4 *Brotherhood of the Holy Trinity Minute Book 7*, 1864, Pusey House, Oxford.

5 'Memories of Liddon addressed in 1899 to J. O. Johnstone', Pusey House, Liddon Papers, V.S.S. Coles.

6 See Peter Groves, 2015, 'Playing football at Mansfield Park: Christian Doctrine and the Local Church', in Shaun Henson and Michael Lakey (eds), *And With All Of Your Mind: Academic Vocation in the Church Today*, Farnham: Ashgate, pp. 49–61.

4

Catechesis as Proclamation: Teaching the Faith Through Preaching

MELANIE MARSHALL

As a girl, I liked to read nineteenth-century novels. From these I absorbed the message that reading novels was the way to an exciting life. The character who reads novels was likely to emerge as the heroine of the story, usually a thrilling tale of thwarted love and joyful consummation. Sermons, meanwhile, seemed to be the reading matter of the unmarriageable sister with the forgettable name. Yet never was there a story more worth reading – and living and telling – than the story of our salvation. It is a story of love thwarted and consummated, of love victorious over betrayal and disaster, of love that never dies. It is, in the name of the 1965 movie, *The Greatest Story Ever Told*. Nonetheless it has always had competition from other stories, stories offering quite different pictures of what the beginning, middle and end of a human life should look like. It suffers from the fact that we have all heard this story lots of times (or think we have). At the same time, it also suffers from the sheer originality of the plot. How should a sensible person react when a hero comes back from the dead?

The work of the preacher is to be the teller of the story of our salvation now, this minute, as it happens. In the mouth of a good preacher, the familiar twists and turns of Christ's story become the current twists and turns of our own lives, present and real and freshly unpredictable. A good preacher makes

Christ's story the only story, the one of such surpassing beauty and truthfulness that all other stories are irradiated (or eliminated) by its light. When preached well, even the supernatural strangeness of Christ's story becomes less an object of scrutiny, and more a lens of possibility. It gestures to a far more distant and glorious horizon than our feeble human vision could reach on its own.

Like any storyteller, the preacher's skill lies in drawing us in. Preaching succeeds exactly to the extent that we are able to see ourselves in the characters, the crises, the resolutions it presents. Like all storytelling, preaching shapes our mental picture of what is possible, what is desirable, what is regrettable, what rings true. It affirms that only love rings true, only fear is to be regretted, only togetherness is to be desired, and that nothing is impossible with God. Like any good story, it also acknowledges the other forces at work. The trolls under the bridge in the preacher's tale are the forces of selfishness and isolation: power, wealth, arrogance, hypocrisy. But we can enter the story with confidence. In the hands of the master Storyteller, good will triumph in the end. And if we have made his story our story, we will triumph like he does – coming back from the dead emphatically included.

In this chapter, we will look at just how preaching tells this tale and draws the listener into it. We'll see how this storytelling helps each hearer to tell and live out the story themselves. We'll consider preaching as first a scriptural, then as a theological, ethical and inspirational form of catechesis. It's often said that the faith is caught, not taught. Sermons can be – and sometimes should be – vehicles for explicit discussion of doctrinal questions, of scriptural data and place for theological debates. But all those features are in the service of the one big compelling narrative arc of the faith: that there was no hope, and then there was hope. Preaching is not a school lesson. It is storytime.

Scriptural Preaching

Most of our formative stories – fairy tales, national epics, jokes – are told first and only later written down. The Gospels of Matthew, Mark, Luke and John are probably based on stories different people told about the life of Jesus. These are the central narrative portion of our tradition, and so a natural basis for the stories preachers tell now. Christ is the head, after all, and Christians are the body. What Christians do, severally and together, is animated by the thoughts, prayers, actions, goals and eternal destiny of the head. All our stories are derived from his story. That is why the Gospel narratives bear telling, and need telling, over and over again. It's also why the Church lays down a universal scheme of Bible passages (the lectionary, from Latin *lectio*, a reading). It ensures we're in step with one another, and that we're reading and preaching about all the parts about Jesus' life, not just our favourite ones.

The story of Jesus is not limited to what we find in the Gospels, though. The lectionary brings together the Gospels with passages of the Old Testament, which shows us earlier parts of the story of what God has done for God's people, before Jesus arrived in the world. It is full of characters and situations that give us a foretaste of what Christ will later be and say and do. We read these alongside letters from the New Testament, where later figures such as St Paul grapple with the meaning and significance of Jesus' life, death and resurrection.

Paul's letters are essentially sermons. So is much of what Jesus says in his earthly life, most famously in the Sermon on the Mount (Matthew 5–7; compare Luke 6.17–49). So, Scripture contains a lot of preaching. Not just that, but much of the preaching within the Bible consists of Jesus or his followers trying to make sense of Old Testament texts now that Jesus is in the picture. Preachers today take up this same work. They carry on explaining the meaning of the Old Testament in light of the New. They also keep on weaving the old stories (including those from the New Testament) into a still newer story of what is happening to us right now. Jesus Christ is the same yesterday, today and always. Christians are still seeking to trace that continuity through a changing world. That is just what John and Paul and Jesus were seeking too. The Bible itself shows us how preaching is done.

Weaving together the old stories with the new stories produces almost limitless ways to engage with Scripture. The earliest Christians, like their Jewish counterparts, were shamelessly creative in the meanings they could extract from their writings. In the same way, modern congregations can be fed by all kinds of readings. Historical readings explain the social and political context of a biblical episode. Metaphorical readings turn the passage back on the hearer, to insert their own experience – Christ is cleansing the Temple: which bits of our 'temples' need 'cleansing'? An odd or rebarbative passage can call forth what we call an apologetic reading, one that explains the place of this line in the whole saving message of Christ. St Augustine was one of the Church's finest readers of the Scriptures. He set us the challenge of finding only love in every word of the Bible – and if we don't find love, to read it again until we do. That should be every preacher's motto.

Like all teachers, a preacher must know their audience. A Godly Play instructor once told us firmly to leave out the descriptions of the plagues of Egypt, as in her experience little boys were so fascinated they would listen to no other part of the story. That said, shock and disgust can sometimes be powerful tools of engagement. When a man is stoned to death for collecting sticks on the Sabbath (Numbers 15.32–36), it offers the preacher an opportunity to engage the moral imagination of the hearer. We cannot enter into a story that has been sanitized out of all recognition. A living and mature faith arises in the Christian community when we're guided in ways to reflect together on the whole of our experience of being human. Pain, anger and confusion have their place, then as now.

Reflecting on Scripture helps the hearer find and take their own place in the saving story that began long ago. It also trains the hearer in how to do their own close reading of Scripture (and anything else) when they need to. Exegesis, interpreting biblical texts, is part of a rich intellectual tradition. But this training is for spiritual and ethical ends. The preacher shows how Christ is present and alive throughout the Scriptures, so that we can be sensitized to all the ways he is present and alive – or absent and silenced – in the world beyond the Scriptures as well.

Theological Preaching

Preaching mainly happens in worship. There, the story of the faith is not only read aloud but acted out. In particular, the main points of our story are described in a summary called the Creed which, in most Christian traditions, the whole congregation recites together. In a Sunday Eucharist, the Creed comes immediately after the sermon. So, as well as explaining the Scriptures that have come before it, the sermon also looks forward. Preaching is a moment of preparation for a powerful communal confession of faith. It strengthens and reminds us of our core beliefs (dogmas) about the person of Christ and the shape of human destiny, so we can be confident in proclaiming them aloud as one body. It is sometimes forgotten that the catechetical value of preaching begins before a word is spoken. We gather as one community. We open ourselves to listening. We respect the authority of the preacher (an authority typically delegated from the bishop). We acknowledge the value of Scripture, and of the traditions of interpretation that shed light on it. We assume the centrality of Christ. All these actions provide tacit assent and affirmation of our shared beliefs. They are reinforced every time we participate in any act of preaching. Even someone who did not understand a word of the sermon would still have been exposed to some crucial aspects of the faith, just by being present.

In a sermon, we are also practising theology as a body. The Church's beliefs are mainly derived from conversations and debates about the Scriptures. So by opening the Scriptures together, the preacher and congregation are doing what the most powerful theologians of the early Church did too. They are making sense of the mixed witness of Scripture in light of all that we know about Christ and his saving work. Of course, the modern preacher is helped by these centuries of tradition. We need not waste time on the false and faulty readings that the Church has dismissed. We can enjoy and explore the many rich possible meanings that the Church has endorsed or permitted. There is a single story – Christ's appearing in a fallen world to bring it fully back to God – but there are lots of ways to tell it. Preaching draws on biography, fiction, anecdote, history and music as places of revelation, shining fresh light on the truth of the one Christian story. Preaching can also explicitly comment on the liturgy, drawing out the symbolism of the baptismal rite or the metaphysical implications of the sacrament. As we hear more sermons, we learn more about how we too can bring ancient Scriptures, later traditions and modern ideas into a fruitful dialogue, always keeping Christ as our guiding principle. Preaching equips the hearer to become his or her own theologian.

Confirmation classes are essential, but for many of us they happened some time ago. Most of us benefit from a regular top-up of Christian learning in manageable portions. Preaching offers this. It reminds us of things we do (or did) know and introduces us to ideas or conflicts we may not have considered. It inspires us to go deeper. Of course, the gospel's simplicity is a large part of its beauty. Being loved is not something we need to have explained with diagrams. But when Christians talk to other Christians, they often use a specialized vocabulary, an established shorthand for some rich and complex ideas. Part of catechesis is to equip believers to become more fluent and confident speakers of the shared theological language of our tribe. Good preaching gradually acquaints the hearer with the traditions and terminology behind Christian beliefs and practice. Everything that happens in the context of worship is meant to equip us to live more Christian lives outside the context of worship. We can explore the faith more deeply and freely if we have started to become conversant with its terms. We can see how the story's beginning ('creation from nothing') fits with its middle ('creation glorifies God') and its end ('God's glory is all in all'). We populate our core beliefs with growing refinement, compassion and understanding. We come to live more and more in the coming reality of Christ.

Ethical Preaching

We have seen how Jesus' story forms the basis for all Christian teaching. But our lives are not exactly like Jesus' life. Jesus can only ever be himself, while we stray far and wide from the selves we are called to be. Our lives are shabby and faulty, painful and confusing, tempting and disappointing. Christ will come again and make everything wholly his own. But for now we live in two parallel realities. There is the redeemed reality that we enter when we are baptized. Then there is a fallen reality in which we are still far from God. In the words of St Paul, Christians are living 'in Adam' and 'in Christ' simultaneously (Rom. 5.12–21). Preaching's ethical task is to bring together these two narratives that are in tension with one another and invite the listener to be the agent of resolving the tension. How can we help close the gap, moving further from Adam and closer to Christ in our words and actions?

A sermon is a weekly confrontation with reality. One of the Church's most famous writers, the Swiss theologian Karl Barth (1886–1968), is supposed to have said that preachers should have the Bible in one hand and the newspaper in the other. Our newspapers are not good news. Even the recipes and fashion-shoots presuppose a horribly unequal world, in which some of us have money for handbags and luxury foods, while others are the victims of suffering, degradation and fear. Political and economic realities are a necessary part of the sermon. As Christians, it is central to our calling that we are taught to see the world more fully as it is, including the worst that humanity is capable of doing and believing. A preacher must tell the world's stories in such a way that the hearer cannot escape their own complicity with the whole network of human cruelty and indifference. The 'right teaching' of catechesis involves learning not just to look at God in the right way. It involves learning to look at the world as God looks at it.

Preaching helps us learn to view human suffering and failure through 'Christ-tinted spectacles'. But that means seeing it not with hatred or fury, the feelings of those who are still far from

God. It means seeing it with pity. We bring before our eyes the sorry truth of human failing so that we can practise the divine skill of forgiveness. We may leave a sermon with new knowledge in the sense of facts – some details about ancient near-eastern society perhaps, or statistics about today's rates of violent crime. Much more important is that a sermon offers knowledge in the sense of 'know-how'. We want to leave a sermon knowing *how*. How to feel about violent crime (pity for both perpetrator and victim). How we are part of it (our own violent thoughts or indifference to poverty). How to act in response to it (prayer for victims, visiting prisoners, donating money to projects that build community). This is the cultivation of a living faith that is true catechesis.

It would be easy to speak as though human frailty and wickedness were toxins that entered our lives through online feeds and news bulletins. But as Jesus points out, it's the things that come from within that defile a person. Preaching tries to tell an honest story about the frailty of individuals as well as societies. Preachers are failures, like everyone else. They are called to have the courage and the faith in God's mercy that lets them voice that failure on behalf of us all. We all know that learning does not happen because one omniscient person lays down the law. It happens when we enter dialogue, acknowledge a common difficulty, and together explore ways to overcome it. Preaching is an important opportunity to face up to the poverty, even dishonesty, of our personal goals and motivations. Yet, in the context of Christian proclamation, we do so in the knowledge that we are loved eternally. Whatever we discover, it cannot destroy us. What it can do is open us up a little further to the transformation God is already working in our lives, giving us an even more joyful story to tell.

Inspirational Preaching

What do we need to participate in the risen life of Christ's Church? We need engagement with Scripture. We need to be able to think and talk in the concepts and language Christians use. We need to be moving towards a more Christ-like life. But more than any of that, we need to want it. No philosopher has so far solved the conundrum of how we make ourselves want something we don't yet want. Luckily theologians have better answers. We can indeed become what we are not, if we have the inspiration of God the Holy Spirit. The Spirit is present in the Church as Christ's gift to us. When the sacraments are celebrated, the Spirit does the transforming work. When Christ is revealed in our reading of the Scriptures, the Spirit suffuses our minds and makes us able to see and understand. Through preaching, too, the Spirit can enter the hearts of believers – inspiring us with hope and consolation, and the courage to decide for Christ.

Conversion stories are often dramatic. St Paul falls to the ground, blinded by the glory of the risen Christ. St Augustine renounces his prideful scepticism, cleansed by the simplicity of a child's voice. The mother of Manche Masemola (1913–28) killed her own daughter to stop her becoming a Christian and 40 years later embraced the gospel herself. But no matter how dramatic the story, conversion is never 'once and for all'. Whether a cradle Christian or a deathbed convert, turning our lives towards Christ is something we each have to do again and again. So, one strength of preaching as catechesis is that it is regular. No matter what happens, the Church will continue reading the Scriptures. We will always be reflecting on their meaning, and that meaning will always be good news. Our busy schedules and our feelings of warmth or coolness towards God this week make no difference to the week-in, week-out proclamation of the truth of Christ.

That regularity provides the preacher with an opportunity not just to inform, but to inspire. Following Christ in our world is not easy. In fact, it is very hard. The threat to the gospel doesn't come from the laughable arguments of the New Atheists. It comes from the unargued principles of market capitalism, an inhumane and exploitative ideology with tentacles in every part of our public and private life. Like many spiritual pitfalls, we are used to it. It seems normal. Our language is suffused with it, our imaginations, our politics. That makes it far easier to go along with this kind of thinking than to stand up to it. Resistance exposes us to ridicule, exclusion, and for some even danger. It means doing without many of the material comforts that we could enjoy by giving in. But we are called to take the harder path, even if the cost is one's life.

It's clear then that Christians will need encouragement. Encouragement is most effective when it is personal, verbal and direct. Our emotions come with us into church, and they drive much of what we do (or don't do) when we go out again. Catechesis is formation of a whole person, feelings and all, so preaching can afford to stir up some feeling for the gospel. It can stimulate a sense of why the truth of Christ is to be desired in the first place. It can express our collective indignation and sorrow at injustice and cruelty. It can inspire us with a sense of how following Christ might yet be possible against all the odds.

Of course, evoking beauty and inspiring love are harder things than correcting falsehood. But they are at least as important. The faith's philosophical coherence or internal logic may be its big attraction for some, enough to capture them heart and soul. For most of us, it is not displays of majesty or intellectual prowess that call forth our compassion and longing. It is vulnerability. Christ comes to us as a naked newborn for a reason. Some of the most effective and memorable sermons include skilful appeals to our gentleness, our patience, our kindness – all fruits of the Holy Spirit, given to us in baptism and waiting to be called forth for service in the world. Some encourage us to imagine what would be lost if the gospel died out, to call our attention to how attached we really are to Christ's message of peace and justice and generosity. A sermon can remind us that Christ has emerged victorious from the unlikeliest conflicts – and by the power of the Spirit in us, can still do so today. The Holy Spirit is given to the Church, Christ's body. One part of the body can stir up another to action.

A Final Thought

Christ's love affirms the infinite worth of everything God has made. It refutes any idea that a person's life or feelings or body can be reduced to a counter in a game for power. It denies that creation is in competition for limited goods, whether material or spiritual. It abhors the abuse and exploitation of one part of creation by another. As Christians, we know this to be true. Yet in a world where it is normal to be selfish, what is there to keep us close to Christ and his message?

Regular exposure to preaching gives us the toolkit to stay faithful to Christ for a lifetime. It teaches us to notice Christ's presence or absence in any text laid before us. It trains us to rationalize and verbalize the truth of Christ. It shows us how to respond with mercy to the world's frailty and our own. It tutors our feelings, so we can be motivated by pity and courage. It brings us together into a community as hearers of one story, so we can go out into the world and tell that story ourselves.

At some point, we are all going to have decide for (or against) Christ. Or, to put it better, we are already deciding for or against Christ, every moment of our lives. Most of this is known only to us and to God. But one day, the outcomes of those decisions will become visible. Jesus promised that things hidden in our hearts would be proclaimed from the rooftops. Through preaching, we gain confidence to proclaim from the rooftops today the truth we will want to inhabit for ever.

5

Sacramental Catechesis:
Enacting Our Source and Aim

JARRED MERCER

Introduction

George Lindbeck, one of the most important theologians of the
past century, helped us to see more clearly what the Church
has always said about Christian doctrine: it is not merely about
truth claims, but the art of living. As he puts it, 'The function of
church doctrines ... is their use ... as communally authoritative
rules of discourse, attitude and action.'[1] By 'rules' he means
not lists of 'do's and don'ts', but something regulative for our
existence – our way of being in the world. That theological talk
depends upon, even grows out of, the lived, practised reality
of the Christian community; that doctrine inhabits social and
political space, and Christians don't think, or speak, or know
in the form of abstract ideas. Christian theology does not exist
in mere abstract conceptual space outside the life lived by and
in the community.

Lindbeck sits in a school of thought called 'post-liberal' or
'narrative' theology (some would call him the most important
figure in this school, though I would argue that his work might
not exist without that of Hans Frei), but none of that really
matters for our purposes. What matters is that whereas these
thinkers might have helped to renew our theological imaginations to recover this way of thinking about our faith and
how we come to know God, theology has always been a lived,

47

performed reality, and no Christian in their right mind would have accepted the divorce made in most of today's seminaries of 'academic' and 'practical' theology and, I would argue, neither should we.

Lindbeck provided a helpful paradigm with which to think about this, what he called a 'cultural-linguistic' approach to Christian doctrine.[2] As languages and cultures form us into certain ways of being in the world and shape our imaginations to see the world in certain ways, so doctrine gives us a grammar for both knowing God and living the Christian life. Communities and cultures are groups of people who share a common past and who interpret their present in light of that common past, and who through their common identity 'anticipate the future by means of a shared hope'.[3]

To participate in catechesis, then, to train others up in the faith, is not to simply teach people to think the right things; it is not to answer difficult questions, and certainly not to provide an apologetic defence for the existence of God. To teach the faith is to train up a certain type of community, a community to exist in the world in a certain way – a people with a shared story and identity, a shared imagination, which unfolds into living towards a certain shared hope. This is so because catechesis, as explored in earlier chapters, is an invitation into new life, a new way of being in the world – living in the hope of the resurrection.

And this type of 'teaching', this invitation, is necessarily sacramental if it is to be truly and genuinely Christian. Why?

There are a few ways to answer this question, and below are three ways in which I think this statement is true, followed by a few practical steps we might take to work towards this truly Christian catechesis.

1 Human beings are sign and meaning makers.
2 Catechesis is transformational, not simply informational, and our transformation takes place through the sacraments.
3 The sacraments enact the entirety of our faith – they accomplish and make 'real' what we are attempting to teach.

Human Beings: Sign and Meaning Makers

Rowan Williams points out that understanding the sacraments as an isolated group of unique actions prescribed by Jesus is problematic. There is something that seems quite arbitrary about this. So discussions about the Eucharist, for example, begin to take place on the level of 'how amazing God's power is to meet us in such a mundane and unnecessary way', or on the other end 'how ridiculous to think that God would choose to meet us in such a mundane and unnecessary way'! As if God willy-nilly just decided, 'I think bread and wine and water sound nice, I'll go there.' But the sacraments are not so arbitrary.[4]

Being an embodied human person is inseparable from sign making and using. We take our common, shared past and do stuff, make things, that reorder our common inheritance and reinterpret ourselves and our current world in light of it. In other words, meaning happens. And we make meaning towards our hopeful future – our aims, goals, or ends – that future shared hope.

This is simply what it means to live in the world as a human being. We live in a world of signs and this is how we make sense of anything. This is what language is and therefore how we speak or think of anything at all, but we must not forget that signs and symbols are made.[5] They are created in the context of a community's actions and interactions. Symbols are not just hanging out and lying around waiting for us to pick up and use them, nor are they simply thought up arbitrarily as metaphors or glosses to help us understand what is 'real' behind them – what they point to. Symbols are made. And in their making, what is real, what is effectual, what is active, what is known and understood, is happening.

All this is to say that it is in the signs, the sacramental actions of our faith, that we are making sense of ourselves – making meaning of ourselves. And not just making sense of ourselves 'on paper'. We are not saying, 'Oh, in the Eucharist, or baptism, or the anointing of the sick, I now see what Christianity is all about – there's the meaning'! As if Christianity were a bit of stale and faded ink on an old piece of parchment. No, in our sacramental action we are making sense of ourselves as if by saying, 'Ah, so that's who we are.' It is a point of self-discovery.

So the sacraments are not just arbitrary instructions given by Jesus, weird stuff we need to do because 'Jesus said so', or strange inexplicable acts of God's power. They are the means, the forms and gifts, given to us to create meaning – to make sense of ourselves in our world today, and tomorrow, and each new day. And, indeed, to create an 'ourselves' in the first place, to make an 'us'. Sacramental action creates us, as through it God establishes the community of the crucified and risen one – today, and tomorrow and each new day.

The fact that humans are naturally sign-makers, that we learn ourselves through sign and meaning making, makes catechesis inherently sacramental. As people exist in communities shaped by the collective making of signs and meaning, we must teach and catechize through a collective commitment to the form, the sacramental, signifying shape of our faith. This is where we are made an 'us', and our formation as a unified people is what we are after in catechesis.

If we are to reach others and train them in the faith our aim must be to provide the framework of signs that actually makes sense of our faith, our world and our lives. In order to understand, teach and pass on our faith we must use the forms that carry the meaning of that faith.

Sacraments: The Means of Our Transformation

Catechesis is sacramental because the aim of catechesis, as we have seen through this book, is the transformation of the entire person into the way of Christ, not simply providing information about the faith, and it is through the sacraments that Christ transforms us and unites us to himself. Again, we are not saying in catechesis, 'Christians are like this', but, 'We are like this, this is who we are, and you're invited to join us.'

In the midst of major reforms in the western Church in the

twentieth century, Pope John Paul II communicated this well in a way that is relevant to Christians in every context and denomination: 'Catechesis is intrinsically linked with the whole of liturgical and sacramental activity, for it is in the sacraments, especially in the Eucharist, that Christ Jesus works in fullness for the transformation of human beings.'[6]

So we can say that catechesis is sacramental because the sacrament is how God catechizes us; the place where God meets us and continues to meet us is in Christ. As the letter to the Hebrews has it, 'in these last days God has spoken to us through his Son' (Heb. 1.2). God shows up in the material world in Christ so that we can come to know God, and God in Christ continues to show up in the earthy, material stuff of our world so that we can know and meet God in the sacramental life of the Church. This is how we know God, this is how God reveals God to us, how God catechizes, or teaches, or forms and shapes us. God teaches us, reveals God's self to us, is made known to us, in the sacrament. Jesus is recognized 'in the breaking of the bread' (Luke 24.35). We should not think that we can be better catechists than God by ignoring the sacramental nature of divine teaching. We should not imagine our pedagogical methods to be above God's!

God is made known in the Scriptures (Luke 24.27), in the teachings of the Church (2 Thess. 2.15; 2 Tim. 2.2), in the face of the poor and suffering (Matt. 25.40), and in our love for one another (1 John 4.11–12), but none of this can be divorced from our sacramental action, because this is simply how humans know and experience things as we are naturally sign and meaning makers. And this is also just how God shows up in our world. It is the particularity of Christ's incarnation that makes sense of all of God's other forms of revelation; that is the fullest expression of God in our lives and world, and the sacramental presence of Christ as the continuation of his incarnation creates the context, makes sense of, the other ways in which we meet God in our lives. The grace and love and mercy of God flow down from the altar and flood the streets so that God is made known in all the world.

There is another important way in which the sacraments

transform us as a community and work to transform the world around us. They are unifying. Giving ourselves over to another in trust, in love, in obedience, is a complete subversion of our self-centred and divisive consumer culture – our rabid individualistic destructiveness that leads to suspicion of one another to the point of anti-trust. If catechesis is not just about right thinking but shaping holy lives, the sacraments are essential in the effort to reshape our lives and imaginations to greet the world as a trusting, generous, self-giving community of love. 'Because there is one bread, we who are many are one body, for we all partake of the one bread' (1 Cor. 10.17).

Our catechesis must involve preparing people and continuing to support people to live in humble and active protest against the forces of division and evil in our society, and for the building up of unity, equality and justice. Nowhere is this seen or has this been seen in history more than in the rich and the poor, the citizen and the foreigner, old and young, saint and sinner, healthy and sick, kneeling together to be united as one in the sharing of Christ's broken body.

This brings me to my third point on why catechesis must be sacramental. The sacrament actualizes, enacts, lives out the faith we are seeking to teach. Through the sacrament, what we teach becomes the reality of our lived experience.

Sacrament – The Living Shape of Our Teaching

Michael Ramsey beautifully wrote of how the Eucharist sits as the framework through which we receive the truth of our faith:

> The Gospel of God is here set forth, since the bread and wine proclaim that God is creator, and the blessing and breaking declare that he has redeemed the world and that all things find their meaning and their unity only in the death and resurrection of the Christ who made them. Here therefore Christian doctrine, with the scriptures and the creeds, finds its true context. Lex orandi, lex credendi ['the law of prayer, the law of belief', or, we believe as we pray].[7]

This is true of the eucharistic rite, because Christian sacramental signs do not just point beyond themselves. When we talk about signs and symbols in a sacramental sense, we are not talking about a sign like a no-smoking or a no-parking sign. These symbols point to a meaning beyond themselves, something that they represent conceptually. When we talk about sacramental signs, we are talking about things that point beyond themselves, that show us who God is and who we are, that teach us what Christ's sacrificial and self-giving love are about, but these signs are also more than pointers guiding the eyes of our minds beyond themselves. In these signs, the very thing that they signify abides. These signs actually make present the thing they point to.

This is why Jesus has always been seen by Christians as the primordial sacrament, the grounding and paradigm for the sacraments. Jesus points beyond himself, he shows us what God is like. If you want to know what God's mercy looks like, what God's power, and love, and grace look like, you look to Jesus. He reveals, he makes God known to us. Jesus also makes us known to ourselves. He is humanity as humanity is intended to be – united to God through union with the divine Word.

But Jesus does not only point beyond himself to show us what God is like. And Jesus does not only point beyond himself to what humanity is really like. Jesus Christ is fully God, and Jesus Christ is fully human. He is divine, he is human – our very nature and God's very nature are truly present in him. Jesus, as a sacramental sign, contains within himself the very thing that he points to: he is the very thing that he signifies – God and humanity.

The sacraments were established as a continuation of Christ's incarnate presence. In particular, we see the Eucharist as a mirror of the incarnation. The fullness of Christ present to us in earthy, material, mundane reality: flesh, blood, bread, wine. Through it we are made Christ's body (1 Cor. 10.17). And so, we are made; and so, our 'meaning making' happens. This is creative action by Christ: establishing, bringing to life a people through a sharing in his death and resurrection. Here we receive our shared, inherited, common past, by which we confront the present, and by which we move towards our hope. Here we receive and make our common identity as a community as we 'anticipate the future by means of a shared hope'.[8]

As Ramsey puts it, 'by sharing in the broken body and the blood outpoured, the disciples will find interpreted both the crucifixion and the whole divine creation whose secrets the crucifixion unlocks'.[9] The whole faith, the whole creation, is here. Catechesis is necessarily sacramental because in the sacrament we are learning, experiencing, receiving the whole of our faith, the whole of ourselves, and the whole of our redemption in Christ. Here we 'find interpreted' the fullness of ourselves and our salvation.

In Christ's life, death, resurrection and feeding we discover ourselves as a community, we learn to read the world, to interpret who and what we are and who our God is, and we see where we are headed. Our whole common life is brought into Christ's sacrifice, and we find – discover – ourselves summed up in Christ's life, death, resurrection and glory.

In the sacraments we are enacting, living out, practising the fullness of our faith: the creeds are put into 'real time' as it were. The Trinity, the incarnation, the grand narrative of our salvation, the making holy of all things, the fullness of the life of the Spirit, the communion of the saints, the forgiveness of sins – all pulling us into the sweetness of the heavenly banquet; into resurrection, life everlasting. The aim and end – our salvation – is here taking place. And nothing teaches us the faith more than its direct enactment in our lives.

Our aim in catechesis must be to share in this creative action that makes us into a people of the crucifixion, of God's self-giving love; a people who themselves are becoming signs of Christ's resurrection life in the world.

Practising Sacramental Catechesis: What Can We Do?

If we are a people becoming the signs of Christ's resurrection in the world, the signs that make us such a people need to be at the centre of all we do and say. This means that in our lives of service, mercy and grace and also in our teaching and preaching we should be drawing people continually towards that sign and meaning making that forms us into who we are and drives us towards our shared hope. Our sermons, for those of us who preach, should be invitations into this reality – invitations to the Eucharist. If we are preparing people for baptism, marriage or confirmation, we should use the rites, knowing that the liturgy moves us towards that point where we are made one as Christ's body – where we are *made*.

One of the most important ways, however, we can catechize through the sacraments and make our catechesis sacramental as it should be is simply by celebrating these signs well; by inviting people into this sign and meaning making, this becoming, with beauty, care, attention, competence and conviction.

I have seen countless priests and pastors be noticeably uncomfortable and awkward when celebrating the sacraments of our faith – especially the Eucharist, though other sacraments also. They look and sound apologetic for doing what they are doing, and sometimes even lost and unprepared, like they do not know what they are doing. If the discomfort does have to do with a genuine lack of knowledge or preparedness, that is of course easily remedied. If we've never learned to enact these signs with precision and depth it is inevitable that we will lack confidence, but we can be open to each other and learn from one another. It is simply unacceptable to work at sermons or other activities with care and diligence and be sloppy and unprepared as we lead people in worship.

I've seen priests stop musicians in the middle of a hymn, yelling up to an organ loft, 'Hey! What verses are we omitting from this hymn again?' (unprepared), as members of the congregation literally giggle. And I've seen a bishop actually crack a joke and laugh his way through a baptism – even at the very point of baptizing the person – because he was unprepared and ill at ease, and it seems that is just how he behaves when in an uncomfortable situation (lack of confidence). At another baptism, a minister went into a long diatribe about the uselessness of baptism, saying, regardless of how ridiculous it may seem to be, 'our Saviour asked us to do some pretty inexplicable things, and so in obedience we baptize people' (lack of depth and understanding). How are others meant to take these central points of our faith seriously if those leading them do not? I assure you, in these kinds of situations, our lack of preparedness, care or attention are the things people will learn and remember. But the celebration of the sacraments is an opportunity both to draw people to the point of meeting Christ and to teach. The first chapter of this book mentions catechesis as beginning with encounter and evangelism and in the school of prayer, and here we have an opportunity to enact and make real these beginnings.

We need to come to the stark realization that this stuff is weird and strange and other. We are talking about the Ultimate Other meeting us in the everyday stuff of life – bread, wine, water, a human person from Nazareth – and it is weird. It is strange, even scandalous, that God comes among us as one of us. But this should be celebrated and rejoiced in, not apologized for. So, let it be weird! People need to be shocked out of their comfortable consumer lives, and they are looking to be, they want to be. If people desire something that looks just like everything else in their life, well, they have it everywhere, and they can skip church and all the Jesus stuff and find it elsewhere. We should relish in the beautiful reality that we have something to gift others outside the restrictive boundaries of our individualist consumer culture – something beyond our self-determining free choice to continually please ourselves and satisfy our every immediate whim. We should not be trying to place another consumer product in the market of comfortability (see Chapter 8). So, let the strangeness of our faith sink in and do not apologize for it. We cannot fetishize the ordinary and become parasitic on consumerism and individualism and all the comfortable idols of our society. We need to be unsettled from it all, and to unsettle others with grace and beauty.

Another issue about confidence and care in sacramental action is that church leaders sometimes think this places them in a box of a particular branch or denomination or tradition in the Church, particularly in my church home of Anglicanism, where people range in belief and practice from evangelical to catholic, and from 'low' church with some songs and a sermon to 'high' church with all the smells and bells in the liturgy. But one does not need to be a Catholic or Anglo-Catholic or high-church Lutheran or anything else to celebrate the Eucharist well (and, by the way, if you are celebrating the Eucharist, you are already catholic in the fullest sense of the word!). At the heart of being the one holy catholic and apostolic Church is celebrating the sacraments, indeed the sacraments are where we are made such a Church. You are not raising your flag for a certain political affiliation in futile Church politics, or even a particular denomination or tradition, by treating God's presence among us in God's chosen vessels to be so present with reverence and awe – you are just being Christian.

If our catechesis, our teaching, our evangelism and passing on of the faith is indeed sacramental, if it really does have the Eucharist at its centre, then offering the Eucharist and drawing people into this meaning making of our faith – this source where we are actually enacted as a community of faith, where we are made one and drawn into our salvation – is not Catholic or Protestant or denominationally specific. It is not a 'worship style' among other 'styles' or preferences, it is just being Christian. This is just our faith.

Conclusion

If catechesis is a sharing in God's activity to make us into a people of the crucified and risen one, of God's self-giving love, a people who themselves are becoming signs of Christ's death and resurrection in the world, then our catechesis will take a sacramental shape. At the core of who we are as people is that we are sign and meaning makers, and the meaning of who we are is made perfect in God-among-us, in Christ with us for our salvation. We touch this reality most fully in the sacramental nature of our faith – continuing to meet God-among-us for our salvation in the ordinary stuff of our lives and world. This of course also changes the meaning of that ordinary stuff and that ordinary world – and it reorients us to that stuff and that world. Christ greets the world with endless, perfect, divine love, and the world can never be the same. Our lives as Christ's followers must always be pointing to that love, always turning others towards it, always becoming signs.

In catechesis we have the opportunity to draw people into this transformative, lived reality of our faith: taking our common story and past, effectuating it in the present, and moving us towards the glory of our shared hope.

Notes

1 George Lindbeck, 1984 [2009], *The Nature of Doctrine: Religion and Theology in a Postliberal Age*, Louisville, Kentucky: Westminster John Knox Press, p. 4.

2 Lindbeck, 1984, p. 4.

3 George Stroup, 1981 [1997], *The Promise of Narrative Theology: Recovering the Gospel in the Church*, Eugene, Oregon: Wipf and Stock, p. 133.

4 See Rowan Williams, 2000, *On Christian Theology*, Oxford: Blackwell, p. 197.

5 Williams, 2000, p. 201.

6 John Paul II, 1979, Apostolic Exhortation *Catechesi Tradendae (On Catechesis in Our Time)*, Catholic Truth Society, par. 23.

7 Michael Ramsey, 1936 [1956], *The Gospel and the Catholic Church*, London: Longmans, Green and Co., p. 119.

8 Stroup, 1981 [1997], p. 133.

9 Ramsey, 1936 [1956], p. 103.

6

Liturgy and Catechesis: Learning Christian Worship

SIMON CUFF

At the end of Matthew's Gospel, Jesus promises us his presence with us always (Matt. 28.20b). Immediately before this, he issues the Great Commission: 'Go therefore and make disciples of all nations, baptizing them in the name of the Father, and of the Son, and of the Holy Spirit, teaching them to observe all that I have commanded you' (28.19–20a). In doing so, he united liturgy and catechesis from the very earliest days of the Church.

Go. Baptize. Teach. These three together make up the unity of our apostolic witness. Go. Baptize. Teach. The Great Commission combines mission, sacrament, liturgy and catechesis. These are the essential ingredients of the Christian life and the proclamation of the gospel.

In this chapter we explore the relationship between liturgy and catechesis, using a broad understanding of 'liturgy' as how we worship and celebrate our faith, and of 'catechesis' as how we teach that faith.

When all is said and done, liturgy is catechesis. How and what we worship is the best tool we have in teaching and preaching the faith – and this worship is what fuels our apostolic mission, our being sent. This interrelationship between liturgy and catechesis is what makes sure we worship the God we teach and teach the God we worship.

Liturgy

Our word 'liturgy' comes from the Greek word *leitourgia*, meaning 'public service' or 'work of the people'. Importantly, this reminds us that whatever our liturgical tradition, we all have a role to play in the liturgy. Whether we are server, engaged in prayer ministry, sub-deacon, acolyte, chorister, or leading the worship-band – we all have a role to play. The liturgy involves, and is the work of, everyone present. The whole of the gathered assembly celebrates the liturgy as much as the celebrant set aside by the community to preside over the particular liturgy of those gathered in worship.

This work of the liturgy extends beyond those physically present to include those who are separated from us physically (by, for example, illness or obligation), but are present with us as fellow members of Christ's body, the Church. It also includes those who have been separated from us physically until eternity, but are still united with us in Christ as fellow members of his body, which not even time can divide.

Our liturgy is also the work of those present *for* those not present. It includes our prayer for all those separated from our worship through illness or obligation, or through lack of faith in or awareness of the gospel. The liturgy is the work of everyone present for all those not present. It's the leaven by which we pray that those outside the gospel might be included in the kingdom, and the means by which we might reach them. The liturgy is the work *of* those present *with* those not present *for* those not present.

Or, to put this another way, the liturgy is the work of Christ. It is not our work but his. As Raniero Cantalamessa, the preacher to the papal household, often begins sermons or addresses: 'Christ is more present to us even now than we are to ourselves.' The liturgy is the culmination of this presence with and for us, and even for those outside that transforming presence. The presence of Christ in the world, and especially in the liturgy, is the means by which those currently outside Christ might be brought into that presence and be transformed. The liturgy is our work, but our work is Christ's.

Here we see how liturgy is related to mission. Contrary to some caricatures or lazy ways of speaking in the modern Church, liturgy isn't an embarrassing block to mission. The claim that liturgy should be avoided because it is confusing or alienating is a misnomer. Bad liturgy confuses and alienates. Liturgy that is the shared language of a group of people who have forgotten how to speak to those outside themselves confuses and alienates.

We know every Christian act of worship has a liturgy – a set of patterns and rituals that are repeated whenever that community meets in order to enable the worship of God. We know too that mission is more than just making new believers say 'yes' to the Christian life. Mission is the whole of the Christian life, or better, mission is what happens when we, the Church, get caught up in what God is already doing in the world and play our part in God's mission.

Understood in this way, our liturgy, however we worship, is intimately related to mission. In the Roman Catholic Church, the fathers of the Second Vatican Council described the liturgy as 'the summit toward which the activity of the Church is directed; at the same time it is the font from which all her power flows'.[1]

Because liturgy isn't a work of our devising, but Christ's – because it's Christ's presence in our liturgies that makes this public work work – liturgy and worship is not an extra to, but the very heart of, mission. Mission is our getting caught up in God's work in the world, and worship our response to it.

By putting mission at the heart of our liturgical celebrations, we remember always that liturgy is supposed to be both part and parcel of the Christian life and should be connected to that life. Through our worship we should gaze on Christ in such a way that others stop and join us in our gaze. Our gazing on Christ in the liturgy should teach others to join us in that gaze.

Catechesis

The meaning of 'catechesis' seems more straightforward, from the Greek 'instruction' or 'instruction by word of mouth'. Deeper in its etymology, as pointed out already in Chapter 2, 'catechesis' is related to 'echo'. Catechesis isn't just teaching in a dry or dusty sense – tweedy academics teaching the faith in ivory towers. Catechesis is teaching that resounds throughout the life of the Church, which reverberates from generation to generation, because real catechesis is nothing less than a sharing in Jesus Christ. As we catechize, the only content of our teaching is the teacher: 'we have one teacher, the Christ' (Matt. 23.10).

Here too we see the relationship between liturgy and catechesis. Catechesis isn't just for the sermon or Sunday school. Liturgy at its best echoes the one who teaches us, when it reflects Christ, when it is more clearly his work. When our worship reverberates with the one whom we worship, we need few words to teach the faith.

We all know the words St Francis never actually used: 'Preach the gospel at all times, where necessary use words.' It doesn't matter that St Francis didn't use these precise words in teaching his brothers how to preach, because they point to something we know to be true. Preaching and teaching the faith is more than just the words we use.

No less an authority than Bananarama confirms this: 'It ain't what you do it's the way that you do it.' It's not just what you do or say in liturgy that matters, in fact the way that you do it matters more. The way we inhabit our liturgy matters, because it's here that we make our words and actions point to the Christ we teach. If we celebrate the sacraments or lead worship with the people entrusted to us on our hearts and at the forefront of our minds, Christ will be made known. This is harder than it sounds.

We also face the ever-present danger of worrying more about the words we say or the actions we perform in the liturgy, than the way we perform them. It matters that our words and actions are authorized and communicate faithfully. However, we can all too easily worry more about getting those words or actions 'right' at the expense of how our celebration communicates the meaning of those words and actions. For our liturgy to be catechetical, one question will occupy us again and again: Is everything we are doing pointing to Christ? Do the words and actions we use point to Christ? Is the way we celebrate the liturgy revealing Christ to those around us, those entrusted to us? There are at least three things that can get in the way of our worship revealing Christ to others: ourselves, idolatry and clericalism.

Ourselves

Our ability to celebrate the liturgy in such a way as to point to Christ has one obvious limitation: us. A lot of what we think we're giving when we're preaching or presiding, in our liturgy and in our worship, is actually not Christ but ourselves – the worship we like, or the things we like to talk about. This is inescapable. Paul's proclamation in 2 Corinthians that 'we do not proclaim ourselves, but Christ Jesus' (2 Cor. 4.5) isn't so much a description, as a challenge.

So much of ourselves gets caught up in our proclamation of Christ. The liturgies and style of worship we favour are so often reflections of our own tastes and preferences, and therefore are limited. How often do our liturgies and our missionary efforts end up attracting 'people like us'?

There's a danger of making ourselves the yardstick of Christ's presence here, and not Christ. The phrases and themes that we think will reveal Christ and build up the body of Christ are often the phrases and themes that once revealed Christ to us.

We know that what revealed Christ to us is subject to time and therefore change. Those of us who have had the responsibility of choosing hymns or songs often find that in one season of our life a certain hymn spoke powerfully of Christ and resounded with the faith, yet now if we hear that same song one more time we'll take early retirement.

Two moments in the twentieth century revolutionized the

way in which liturgy was celebrated: the liturgical movement within established denominations and the charismatic movement across the global Church. The Second Vatican Council's *Sacrosanctum Concilium*, written in 1963, demonstrates one aim of the liturgical movement, that elements in our liturgies that 'have suffered injury through accidents of history are now to be restored to the vigour that they had in the days of the holy Fathers'.[2] Both the liturgical movement and the charismatic movement reinvigorated worship across the Church. However, even these reinvigorating movements demonstrate the tendency for worship that once spoke powerfully of Christ to speak more and more of itself. Such worship quickly became staid, speaking less powerfully of Christ and more of its own patterns and motifs.

Across the Church today we are seeing new liturgical movements which are once again reinvigorating worship by restoring some of the words and actions these earlier movements found no longer spoke so powerfully of Christ.

Any means of encountering Christ, all forms of worship, can be welcomed if the yardstick by which we judge them isn't ourselves, or our preferences and predilections, but Christ. The yardstick of any liturgy is its ability to mediate to us the presence of Christ.

All too easily we tell ourselves that we worship in the way that has always spoken of Christ, and that we are the bastions of continuity. As a catholic Anglican, this is also true of my own ecclesial tradition. However, Anglo-Catholicism has always been a reinvigorating movement. Our forefathers and mothers set out to reform the Church of England and its worship to speak more powerfully of Christ. Anglo-Catholics were once the reformers and the innovators. Today, we all too easily cling to worship that is staid and seek to defend what once spoke to us of Christ. We find ourselves in exactly the position of those our forebears challenged and set out to refresh. The vocation of all Christians, and the vocation with catholic Anglicanism especially, is ever to reinvigorate and place Christ at the centre of our worship.

We see here that Christ's command to remember that he

will be with us always, after giving us the command in the Great Commission to go, baptize and teach is no accident. Our mission, our celebration of the sacraments, our catechesis all too quickly go astray without constant vigilance to ensure that Christ is at their centre, that Christ is being remembered.

The task of restoring vigour to our liturgy is not just a one-off or once in a generation challenge, it's an ever-constant task to ensure that Christ is the focus of our worship and not us. It is an ever-constant task to ensure that it is God that we are worshipping and not our favoured form of 'worship'. It is the way in which we inhabit these liturgies, these words and actions, that is vital. Are we doing so in a way that reinvigorates those around us, that speaks powerfully of the refreshment found only in Christ?

Idolatry

This is harder than it sounds. The danger of worrying more about the words we say or the actions we perform in the liturgy, than the way we perform them is difficult to avoid. Even worse, we can all too easily mistake those words or actions, designed to help us encounter Christ, for that encounter. We lock Christ and ourselves into certain words or liturgical habits, and we don't let the presence of Christ transform and reinvigorate the words we use and the actions we perform.

We're reminded here of the ever-present danger of idolatry. Again and again Scripture warns us of this danger, which runs deep in the human condition. Our propensity to make idols for ourselves can even extend to the things we hold most dear in our Christian lives, and the liturgy is no exception.

Stephen Fowl notes the essential role of catechesis in helping prevent the symbolic actions of our worship and liturgy becoming idolatrous: 'if Christians' catechetical practices are not in good working order, then it becomes ever more likely that their symbolic practices will not signify properly. Indeed should the symbolic role of these practices become detached from their catechetical moorings, they risk becoming free-floating images that lose their precise symbolic force ... Catechesis is one way of maintaining symbolic actions so that they continue to do their work.'³

Moreover, the liturgy – the summit of God's activity and presence in the world – trains us to look for God's Spirit at work elsewhere in creation, or it should. It is all too easy for our worship and liturgy to become an idol if we start seeing God's presence and activity in these moments alone. We can become so fixated on the words and actions we use that we fail to recognize that they are supposed to help us to see more of God's work in the world, not less.

All too easily our liturgy, our way of celebrating the sacraments becomes an idol. Our worship becomes worshipped. We cling too rigidly to the form of worship that's helped us or has made us aware of the presence of God in our midst. And we're blind to the insights of other Christians as to how those not already worshipping with us might encounter God's presence in different ways – and how we too might be missing out on new ways of deepening our awareness and encounter of the divine.

By remembering liturgy is the shared language of every Christian community coming together in the worship of God, we are less likely to make an idol of our own liturgy and more likely to have our worship enriched by sharing in the patterns and practices that have enabled others to encounter the presence of God. We are also more likely to be open to transforming our Church's life in ways that will aid our catechesis and speak more powerfully of Christ.

Our worship will be catechetical if it's always pointing to Christ, if we as those celebrating the liturgy and devising forms of worship always have this end in mind.

Clericalism

Before thinking about how we ensure the way we inhabit the liturgy speaks more clearly of Christ, it's worth recognizing another danger we face as Christians.

We've said repeatedly that the yardstick of our liturgy should be Christ. If the liturgy is to be catechetical, if it is to teach the one we worship, we need always to ensure that it speaks of Christ to those gathered to share in our liturgy and to worship. All well and good. This sounds great, but what does it mean for a liturgy to speak powerfully of Christ? Who's to be the judge?

We've all had moments in our life, however rare and fleeting, where we have been bowled over by God's presence. We've also all hopefully encountered congregations and communities where Christ's presence is tangible – a group of people who are on fire with the love of the Lord. That fire of which *Sacrosanctum Concilium* hopes will be stoked by the Eucharist: 'of the covenant between the Lord and man (which) draws the faithful into the compelling love of Christ and sets them on fire'.[4]

We've also all, probably, encountered churches and communities where the opposite is the case. Part of this stems from the way we celebrate our liturgies. Are we inhabiting them in such a way that we stoke the renewal of that fire; that we strengthen the covenant between the Lord and his people which draws them into that love. Or has our fire gone out; are we staid? Has our celebration of the liturgy become routine or run of the mill? Have we stopped allowing ourselves to be transformed by Christ so that we might speak more clearly of Christ to those around us?

A community gathered around a liturgy that speaks powerfully of Christ will speak for itself. Our yardstick should be how powerfully Christ's presence is recognized in the community which has been entrusted to us – where God has placed us. How powerfully does our liturgy speak of Christ to that group of people? Inevitably, this will mean some element of diversity.

Liturgies that speak powerfully of Christ to one parish or congregation will speak differently to those who, for whatever reason, cannot hear Christ in the same way. This isn't hopeless relativism but charism. Many gifts, but the same Spirit (1 Cor. 12.4). It's long been known that congregations and communities each have a charism of their own. If a community is confidently living out that charism, the particular calling of that community and Christ's presence will be tangible. The ability of our liturgy to speak Christ in the community entrusted to us, to make known his presence, is the yardstick of all our liturgical effort.

Too often, however, we fall foul of a kind of clericalism or the personality cult of Christian leadership. The voices and opinions of other clergy or notable Christian figures become our yardstick, rather than how powerfully the presence of Christ resonates in the community entrusted to us.

It's been a feature of Pope Francis' papacy to speak against such clericalism which homogenizes the laity, extinguishes the prophetic flame with which we are to bear witness, forgets that the visibility and sacramentality of the Church belong to the whole people of God.[5]

We fall foul of this kind of clericalism when we celebrate the liturgy not with the people of God given to us in mind, but with one eye over our shoulder as to what our brother and sister clergy or Christian celebrity might make of this or that act of worship or church service. We can find ourselves wearing and doing some remarkable things because we want to be seen to be the real deal to our fellow clerics and Christians, and quite forget that it means nothing if what we're doing isn't bringing those who have been entrusted to us closer to Christ. Enabling a powerful encounter with Christ might sometimes mean doing less of what is expected of notable Christians in our tradition and getting out of the way more to allow Christ to speak through us. A liturgy that might speak powerfully of Christ in one context, might look facile in ours or recherché in another. Christ must ever be our judge and standard of judgement – not us.

Priestly Sacrifice

So, finally, how do we ensure that we do not preach ourselves, that we can and do get out of the way, to allow Christ to speak as we celebrate the liturgy? How do we inhabit our forms of worship so that they speak ever more powerfully of the one who teaches us and is the content of our teaching?

Much ink has been spilled about the nature of the sacrifice at the heart of our liturgy. However one views that sacrifice, we know that Christ's sacrifice meets ours in our worship: 'through him we offer you our souls and bodies to be a living sacrifice' as the Church of England's Common Worship has it.[6]

It's here that the way in which we celebrate the liturgy bears fruit. We're called upon to be a living sacrifice – to put our all into it. Our tone, our voice, our posture, our behaviour, our interactions with servers and fellow-worshippers – all of these are capable of being used by God to speak powerfully to his people. And all are liable to get in the way and render the liturgy less capable of speaking powerfully of Christ. If we are impatient with others in the sanctuary, we put a stumbling block in front of those gathered for worship. If we make our liturgy seem run of the mill, or if we rush in from one appointment and out to the next, all of these ways of being can get in the way of an encounter with Christ.

Sacrosanctum Concilium again instructs that 'the treasures of the Bible are to be opened up more lavishly, so that richer fare may be provided for the faithful at the table of God's word'.[7] If we're run of the mill or rushing or short-tempered in our celebration, we're not putting on a lavish feast. All too often we offer liturgies of skimmed milk, when we're called upon to serve double cream.

Catechetical Worship

Worship that is lavish, to which we've given our all, which has been reinvigorated and is reinvigorating, will speak powerfully of Christ. But we might be thinking, such worship sounds exhausting. It's impossible, given all the demands on our time, to make every act of worship such a feast. It's nice to have Christmas dinner once a year but if we cooked and ate it three times a day, we'd never have time to do anything else, and we'd quite quickly be sick of it.

Here we see the importance of good catechesis. A community that has learned to look for Christ in the liturgy and is ever open to being transformed by him will make a feast out of the most meagre of our liturgical offerings.

I want to end by sketching a vision for how we devise and celebrate liturgies that speak powerfully of Christ and teach and inspire the faith, so that those worshipping with us might be more aware of the Christ who has called us all into his Church to worship him.

First, liturgy is the work of everyone – not just clergy or experienced worship leaders. The greater the participation of the whole community in devising liturgy, the more likely it will speak powerfully of Christ to the particular community at large. Moreover, those devising worship are formed and shaped by Christ as they devise it, and the more lavish each and every celebration can become. It's impossible to cook Christmas dinner on your own every week, but it's a lot easier when others play their part.

Second, Christmas dinner every week would soon cease to be Christmas dinner. Liturgical catechesis is year-long. We don't teach or preach the entirety of the faith in each and every celebration. Nor do we serve the same menu again and again. The lectionary and liturgical year are gifts to our catechesis, enabling us to focus on making a particular part or theme of the Christian life speak more powerfully of Christ. A simple theme expanded on throughout the liturgy will speak more clearly and resolutely to people of all ages and abilities. Here the power of symbol and the importance of sacrament are obvious as both go beyond the limited capacity of our words to communicate and express the depths and mystery of faith. Those symbols in which we know Christ is present speak more simply and powerfully than we can ever hope to.

Third, liturgical catechesis should speak to people of all ages and abilities. The content of the Sunday school should be as nourishing to the children as the content of the sermon to those listening. Liturgical catechesis is lifelong. A community that ever seeks to be transformed by Christ, ever seeks to hear his voice more powerfully, will be used to being challenged and transformed by Christ into Christ.

Liturgical catechesis is lifelong. Key moments in the Christian life will be celebrated lavishly as moments pregnant with the possibility of divine encounter – births, marriages, deaths, confirmations, first communions, and so on. These will never be run of the mill. We will always be asking ourselves how these can speak more powerfully of Christ.

And finally, liturgical catechesis is not just lifelong, but fills the whole of the life of the worshipping community. Waking, eating, sleeping will be marked by moments that offer the possibility of teaching and encountering Christ. Rediscovering the potential of prayers before meals and night prayers at bedtime, not simply repeating prayers and liturgies of the past, but seeking here too to find ways and means of speaking more powerfully of Christ.

All of this can be seen in how our teacher teaches, by looking closely at what Christ does in the institution of the Eucharist. Every Eucharist is done 'in remembrance of him'. Every Eucharist is celebrated by Christ, points us to Christ, and strengthens us in Christ.

If we look more closely at what Christ did in the institution of the Eucharist, it helps us avoid some of the dangers we've spelled out here and to celebrate the liturgy in a Christ-like way so that it speaks ever more powerfully of Christ.

Jesus doesn't create a liturgy from scratch nor does he repeat without alteration the liturgies of the past. Rather, he celebrates the liturgy of Passover, and the daily Jewish tradition of prayers over meals, and transforms those liturgies so they speak more powerfully of him, so that what he is about to do for us and for our salvation is at their centre.

Our worship and liturgy can be its most catechetical when it points most clearly to Christ. When we, like Christ in the institution of the Eucharist, neither simply repeat the past nor restart from scratch – but enter into the great liturgical traditions and celebrations that make up our Church today, always making sure they still speak as powerfully of Christ as they did in their devising, always making sure that Christ is as much at their centre for those outside the Church as he was for us when we first began worshipping in this way. If our worship and celebration of the sacraments ever speaks of Christ anew, we won't be far off in our liturgy and in our catechesis and, more importantly, neither will he.

Notes

1 *Sacrosanctum Concilium* 10, 4 December 1963, available at www.vatican.va/archive/hist_councils/ii_vatican_council/documents/vat-ii_const_19631204_sacrosanctum-concilium_en.html, accessed 28 May 2018.

2 *Sacrosanctum Concilium* 50, 4 December 1963, available at www.vatican.va/archive/hist_councils/ii_vatican_council/documents/vat-ii_const_19631204_sacrosanctum-concilium_en.html, accessed 28 May 2018.

3 S. Fowl, 2019, *Idolatry*, Waco, TX: Baylor University Press, pp. 39–40.

4 *Sacrosanctum Concilium* 10, 4 December 1963, available at www.vatican.va/archive/hist_councils/ii_vatican_council/documents/vat-ii_const_19631204_sacrosanctum-concilium_en.html, accessed 28 May 2018.

5 See especially Pope Francis, 19 March 2016, 'Letter of His Holiness Pope Francis to Cardinal Marc Ouellet, President of the Pontifical Commission for Latin America', available at: https://w2.vatican.va/content/francesco/en/letters/2016/documents/papa-francesco_20160319_pont-comm-america-latina.html, accessed 26 June 2018.

6 The 1662 Book of Common Prayer contains the same idea: 'And here we offer and present unto thee, O Lord, ourselves, our souls and bodies, to be a reasonable, holy, and lively sacrifice unto thee.'

7 *Sacrosanctum Concilium* 51, 4 December 1963, available at www.vatican.va/archive/hist_councils/ii_vatican_council/documents/vat-ii_const_19631204_sacrosanctum-concilium_en.html, accessed 28 May 2018.

7

Catechesis and the Cultivation of Virtue

JONATHAN JONG

What are Virtues?

Unless you have skipped right to this chapter, bypassing the others, you will already have encountered our insistence that Christian catechesis is about learning how to live. By this, we mean the quite literally mundane thing of how to live in the world, and especially with other people. The Christian life is, like human life more generally, a social and political life. The word 'political' scares some people, but I am using it in quite a broad way to refer to life in a society: it comes from the Greek word *polis*, meaning 'city', though I am certainly not assuming that all societies are urban.

Learning how to live in the world does, of course, involve learning how (and even what) to think, as well as learning what and how to do the sorts of things Christians regularly do in churches and chapels. But in the end, the Christian faith is a living and lived faith, and most of life happens outside classrooms and churches: most of life happens at home and in the workplace and on public transport and in queues. This is where most humans live out most of their lives, and is therefore where Christians have to live also.

The fact that the Christian life is like human life more generally is no accident: to be a Christian is nothing more or less than to be human. Perhaps it is presumptuous for us to say, but Christians do say that we have some idea about what it means to be truly human. We get this idea from Jesus, who we believe to be the image of true humanity. It is not just that Jesus – in his teachings and in the way he himself lived – is a good example, even a paragon of humanity. Christians also believe that we, through our baptism, participate in Jesus' true humanity. The Bible has many ways of talking about this: it speaks of us being 'in Christ' (e.g. Rom. 12.5; 2 Cor. 5.17) or even being 'the Body of Christ' (e.g. 1 Cor. 12.27; Eph. 4.12).

None of this is to say that Christians are, on the whole, any good at living true human lives. Indeed, the history of the Church can be written as a catalogue of conspicuous failures to live up to our baptisms, interjected by the occasional bright spot of founding schools and hospitals, alleviating poverty and pain, and speaking out for the marginalized and disenfranchized. If we have any special insight on how to live, it is the insight gained through prayerful failure, the kind of learning that is most like a child stumbling her first steps into the arms of her father.

Fortunately, Christians do not have to rely only on other Christians' insight; indeed, we have always been willing to find truth and wisdom wherever they may be found. As our Old Testament was a Jewish text before it also became a Christian one, we obviously owe a lot of our moral philosophy to Jewish thought, especially in the Law and the Prophets. Beyond the Bible, arguably the biggest influence on the way Christians have thought about what is sometimes called the good life has been ancient Greek philosophers like Plato and especially Aristotle.

This chapter will not fall very far from this particular tree, as it concerns the relationship between catechesis and the cultivation of virtue, and what catechesis has to look like if it's going to contribute to Christian moral life. In the West, the idea of virtue was certainly first developed by Plato and Aristotle. Its abiding influence in the Church can be attributed in large part to the work of Thomas Aquinas in the thirteenth century. (In the East, the virtue tradition has Mencian and Confucian roots, but that goes beyond the scope of this chapter.)

According to the tradition of Plato, Aristotle and Aquinas,

virtues are habits or dispositions. This is often understood as dispositions of behaviour, but it is important to remember that there are also habits of thoughts and desires and emotions, which can affect our behaviour. More narrowly, virtues are good habits, whereas bad habits are called vices. The cultivation of virtues is therefore the acquisition of good habits. One influential way of thinking about the acquisition of habits is that it is very much like learning a skill, like riding a bicycle or writing in cursive.

What are the Virtues?

Having been introduced to the distinction between virtues and vices, it is natural to wonder how we can determine what counts as a good or bad habit. On one hand, this seems an easy task. We can all broadly agree that courage, truthfulness and kindness are good, and also that greed and hubris are bad. To be sure, we might disagree – between individuals, across cultures and over time – on the emphases we put on these in different situations, but the diversity of moral opinion ought not to be overstated, especially at the level of basic values.

To say that there is broad agreement about what the virtues (and vices) are is one thing; it is quite another to come up with a definitive list, and another thing again to explain why some things are on the good side of the list while others are on the bad side. Ever since Aristotle, until quite recently – some time in the eighteenth century – the usual way of thinking about good habits and bad habits is to think in terms of ends, which are a thing's goals or purposes. There began to be scepticism in the eighteenth century about whether it makes sense to talk about things, including people, having ends. I think it does.

It is easiest to start by thinking about tools. For example, what makes a toaster a good toaster is that it reliably toasts bread, preferably evenly and to the desired extent depending on your chosen setting. A toaster that leaves half the slice cold, while burning the other half would not be a good toaster; nor would one that always toasted the bread to the same extent regardless of your chosen setting. Whether or not a toaster can boil an egg is, though handy, not relevant to how good a toaster it is. A toaster that never toasts bread is not a toaster at all, but a toaster-shaped ornament. The general principle at work is that what makes something good depends on the thing that it is and what it is for.

An analogy can be made in the case of things that are not tools, like trees or giraffes. Their end is to be alive as the things that they are. In quite the same way that a toaster that doesn't make toast – a broken toaster, say – isn't really a toaster, a dead tree is not really a tree, nor is a dead giraffe really a giraffe. So, one of the ends of being a tree or a giraffe is to remain alive. Trees and giraffes have different ways to remaining alive: trees photosynthesize with their leaves and absorb water and nutrients through their roots, while giraffes eat leaves from tall trees and stoop down low to drink water. And so, these activities belong on the good side of the ledger. We might also think beyond the individual tree and giraffe to the species or the ecosystem to which they belong: after all, certainly in the case of the ecosystem, the health of the collective does affect the health of the individuals. Thus, the tree's growing leaves that become food for the giraffe, and the giraffe's leaving droppings that fertilize the tree can also be considered good.

Human beings are rather a lot like giraffes, both being animals. Like a giraffe's, a human being's flourishing has a great deal to do with biological activities, but there is more to human flourishing than biological flourishing. Giraffes are not the most social animals in the world, though they do tend to live in herds. In contrast, human beings flourish best in families, friendships and societies. The Bible recognizes this from the very beginning, saying in the book of Genesis that it is not good for us to be alone. Social scientists have also always recognized this, and have documented the adverse effects of social deprivation on children and adults alike. It is good for a human being to be able to enjoy relationships. We use many words to describe good relationships. Christians are particularly enamoured of love as a characteristic of good relationships.

The supreme importance of love is obvious from the witness of Scripture. Jesus says repeatedly to love God and our neighbours, and even our enemies (e.g. Matt. 5.44; Luke 6.35, 10.25–28; John 13.34); he even calls love of God and neighbour the greatest commandments, on which 'hang all the law and the prophets' (Matt. 22.37–40; Mark 12.29–31). This prioritization of love is then echoed elsewhere in the New Testament (e.g. Rom. 13.8–10; 1 Cor. 13.13; 1 John 4.7–8) and throughout the history of Christian moral theology thereafter.

Throughout the history of moral thinking, theological or otherwise, Christian or otherwise, people have come up with different lists of virtues. This is not the place to debate them. It is probably enough for us to know the general principle that virtues are those habits that promote human flourishing, both individual and social; and the Christian prioritization of love as the most excellent of the virtues (Aquinas, *Summa Theologiae* II-II, Q23, A6; 1 Cor. 13.13).

For good measure, it might also be useful to have a list of the seven virtues that have enjoyed the most discussion among Christians through the centuries. Of the seven, four are called cardinal virtues, from the Latin word meaning 'hinge' because they are the basic virtues on which other good habits turn. The cardinal virtues are justice, fortitude (or courage), temperance and prudence (or wisdom) to guide the other three. Love is not among the cardinal virtues: instead, it is among the theological or divine virtues, which also include faith and hope. These three are called theological virtues because they are primarily directed at God – love for God, and faith and hope in God – and also because they are believed to be infused by God into us, who do not possess them naturally. This is not to say that we are not, having been infused with these virtues, responsible for exercising and cultivating them in ourselves and one another. To the contrary, it would be an abuse of God's gift to us if we did not let it grow in us.

Virtues as Skills

Spanning about one quarter of the whole, Part Three of the Catechism of the Catholic Church – arguably the Roman Catholic Church's most important catechetical guide – is devoted to 'Life in Christ', which covers what might be called moral theology or theological ethics. Article 7 of this section of the Catechism is about the virtues, and it includes the list of cardinal and theological virtues also given earlier. It goes on to explain, in brief, what each virtue means. Clearly, the Church assumes that it is important for Christians to learn what the virtues are. Perhaps it is: but it is also the least interesting aspect of what it means to teach and learn how to live in Christ. To know what the virtues are is one thing; to acquire and exercise them is another thing altogether. As the fourth-century Christian philosopher Lactantius put it, 'virtue is thus not knowing good and evil; it is, rather, doing good and not doing evil'.[1]

The Catechism also says that virtues are 'acquired by education, by deliberate acts and by a perseverance ever-renewed in repeated efforts'. The Church tends to emphasize the first means of virtue acquisition – education – whether through preaching, small group discussions, or books like this one. The Church seems to do less about the other two, presumably leaving them up to individual Christians to practise in their own time. This seems to me to be a mistake.

There is a long tradition of thinking of virtues like skills, which makes sense of the Catechism's prescription of deliberate and repeated effort. Practise makes morally perfect, if you like. Aristotle likened the cultivation of virtue to athletic training, and others have used the examples of learning how to play a musical instrument or a game like chess. I like to think of it like learning a new language. The mastery of each of these skills takes practise. The importance of repetition is most obvious when it comes to the development of physical or practical ability, but memory for information – the way a piece is meant to sound, the rules of a game, the meanings of words – is also improved by repeated exposure and exercise.

Repetition is necessary in the development of a skill into an expertise, but it is not sufficient. As memory researchers have known for decades, it is easier to remember information that can be coherently organized within what we already know: in other words, understanding promotes memory, and this is also true for other kinds of skills. Understanding why 1.d4 is a good opening move in chess or how notes form chords in music also allows for creativity in how we play, which in turn makes us more versatile players. And as every poet knows, the conventional meanings of words can be expanded, and the accepted rules of grammar can be bent to great effect. The ability to play skilfully with language requires more than a large vocabulary and infallible knowledge of grammatical rules: it requires familiarity with the literary and cultural context of one's audience, and benefits from historical and etymological knowledge. Something like this is true of virtue too. The exercise of virtue admits creativity, sometimes to the chagrin of reactionary moralizing forces. The catechetical implications for this are therefore relatively clear. To the extent that when we compartmentalize teaching liturgy, doctrine, ethics and politics, we are failing to promote understanding of how Christian beliefs and practices fit together. This impedes the cultivation of virtue.

All these skills – but perhaps especially language – are best learned with others. We can learn a new language from reading books, or watching instructional videos, which might be better for pronunciation. But there is no substitute for a good teacher who will speak with us, making corrections and suggestions when necessary, always being sensitive to our current levels of proficiency. Better still is the teacher who eventually encourages us to leave the classroom, even to immerse ourselves in a community of other speakers of the language with whom we can converse and from whom we can learn. This kind of teaching is what the Church – her leaders, but also as a community of Christians more broadly – needs to get better at. This too is a skill that requires practise, and we shall later consider some practical suggestions. But first let us return to the idea that love is a virtue, and therefore that learning to love is like learning a skill.

The thing about skills is that they involve actions and outcomes. They involve intentions too, of course: the intention to score a goal or play Bach's 29th Goldberg variation or open with a queen's gambit or write a book chapter about the cultivation of virtues. But they cannot only involve intentions: we cannot claim to be playing Bach's 29th Goldberg variations successfully if we are unable to pull off his arpeggios, no matter what we intend. This point about the moral incompleteness of intentions – and psychological states more generally – also serves as a correction against the common idea that love is a feeling, and one that *ipso facto* makes an action good. Not only do feelings fail to cover a multitude of sins, but love is not, Christianly conceived, a feeling.

It turns out to be rather difficult to specify what actions love entails. We can say that to be courageous is to be willing to face our fears, especially to accomplish some other good. We can say that to be truthful is to refuse to lie or mislead, being careful that we say what we mean and that what we mean is not itself false. Love seems too broad for this kind of analysis, and perhaps it is. Of course, as we have already touched upon at the beginning of this chapter, we have a paradigmatic model of love in Jesus, who in turn shows us something about the mutual self-giving that is the life of the Trinity.

From Jesus' teaching and example, we learn that love involves self-denial for others' sake, such as when he says 'Love your enemies, do good to those who hate you, bless those who curse you, pray for those who abuse you' (Luke 6.27–28), and indeed when he lays down his own life for us. Christians have also often turned to St Paul's first letter to the Corinthians for guidance, where he says that love is kind and patient, and is not envious or resentful, and so forth. Even if it is still difficult to identify the loving thing to do in any given situation, these examples and expositions of love give us a litany of skills to practice.

Teaching Virtues

Whether we like it or not, quite a lot of teaching that happens in and around churches looks like the kind of teaching that happens in school classrooms and university lecture halls. This is to say that teaching as it typically happens in churches does not look very well suited for the teaching of practical skills. Indeed, we do not teach very many practical skills in church, except perhaps when we teach people how to pray. If we are blessed indeed, our Bible study groups might involve more than the transmission of content about Palestinian geography or Greek etymology, but actually learning how to engage with texts.

There is one other notable exception to this generalization, which should be especially familiar to all ordained ministers. As a curate, a newly ordained deacon or priest begins to minister to her congregation under the supervision and guidance of a more experienced priest. At its best, a curacy is a time for developing good habits of various kinds, liturgical, pastoral and so forth. This happens through the novice watching the experienced priest; through the latter's explanations of how things are done and why they are done in such a way; through the novice's own attempts to fulfil her various new responsibilities, and her willingness to ask questions and admit weaknesses; and through the experienced priest's encouragement and advice. When the curate is ready to move on, perhaps to become a vicar somewhere, not only should she have developed several good habits (and rooted out bad ones), but she should also be more able to encourage, evaluate, and correct herself as well as others.

Now, I do not think it necessary for priests to take on the additional duties of training every individual member of their congregations as though they were curates. Not only would this be unduly clericalist, as if lay people are not able to lead in the work of catechesis, but it is also redundant. Most churches already do the sorts of things that can – with some modification – promote the cultivation of virtue.

Most churches run on volunteers, who sacrifice their time

and energy to enable the church's ministry and mission; many churches also organize opportunities for their members to volunteer elsewhere, at soup kitchens, night shelters for the homeless, and so on. Most churches also run on charitable giving and would simply fold without the largesse of their members; many also redistribute money, both to needful members of the church or to others outside the church. In other words, there is already virtue to watch, in which to participate, and from which to learn.

Churches also already offer plenty of opportunities to discuss real-life issues, especially in the context of preparing for different things that happen in church like weddings, baptisms, confirmations and funerals. The use of the word 'catechism' to refer to the teaching that happens in preparation for baptism is very ancient, and we still associate catechism and baptism very closely, though in practice we are nowadays more likely to catechize a candidate for confirmation than one for baptism, given the common practice of baptizing infants. But we are missing a trick if we do not task the catechizing of the infant's parents as seriously as we do that of a teenage confirmand. Similarly, while our meetings with couples to be married tend to be practical and those with grieving families tend to be pastoral, both can also be opportunities for teaching and the cultivation of virtue. Better still if our close encounters with parents and couples and families do not cease after the services in question. Parenthood, marriage and bereavement are – like workplaces and trains – places where real human lives take place, and therefore where Christian lives ought to too.

Perhaps less common are systems of accountability. Churches in the Catholic tradition do practice the sacrament of reconciliation, in which the penitent confesses their sins, and asks for advice and absolution. Evangelical churches tend to avoid this sort of thing, but do often encourage a more informal version within small groups. In either case, there are already habits of being honest about our weaknesses, and of offering advice and encouragement in light of such honesty.

The trouble is that we do not tend to think of these practices as catechetical, and therefore fail to be mindful of the opportunities, for example setting, moral teaching, encouragement and advice, that are available. How often do we talk to our volunteers – our churchwardens, sacristans, flower team, hospitality team, and so forth – about the work that they do in terms of exercises in virtue? How often do we encourage those who give financially to the church to think of this as practise for broader generosity? It is, after all, easy to give time and money to one's own community: but the demands of love are that we give of ourselves even to our enemies. All of this is just to return to the point made earlier about the importance of understanding, of unifying various things we know into a coherent whole.

The Church as a Place for Learning

The word 'catechesis' implies teaching by talking. And for the most part, this is fine, even in the context of virtues. We can talk about the virtues, what they are and why we think them virtuous. We can discuss examples of virtuous behaviour, and confess to each other our failures to live up to them, and encourage one another to do better. We can exchange recommendations for how to practise virtue, and advice on how to overcome vice. But we should not stop there.

It is common knowledge that some environments are more conducive to learning than others. This is why we have schools and universities, and indeed seminaries, monasteries and convents. They exist as crucibles of learning and, in the latter cases, of Christian discipleship. The parish church is not a convent, nor should it be; but it is and should be a society, so arranged to bring the best out of people, out of each other. This is especially important because the world where life happens – the workplaces and supermarkets and parent-teacher meetings and social media platforms – turns out to be a difficult place to practise being human.

As Chapter 8 of this book points out, every day in the world, our desires are being shaped by advertisers looking to sell us whatever simulacra of happiness their corporate masters have conjured up on the backs of people too desperate to know or care that they are being exploited. Every day, our habits are being formed by demands to compete, to outperform others and even ourselves, to grow and grow, faster and faster, ever world without end. If people are not competition, then they are consumers or 'human resources' to be leveraged for competitive advantage. Even our children are not exempt from this mad culture: every year a new parenting fad, every year more pressures placed on parents – mothers especially – to do this thing and not that thing for the sake of a handful of additional IQ points or something else equally inane.

This is not a good place to learn how to live, though we all do have to live here, and not only that but also to bring life here. Those of us who minister in urban settings may have observed that people regularly come into our churches to sit quietly, and perhaps even to pray. The Church has always been a refuge from the world. The people who come in eventually head back into the world, of course, and this is only right. The Church does not – should not – offer escapism: we are sent into the world just as Christ was. What the Church should offer is an environment in which Christians can be prepared for life in the world, and this does take more than didactic teaching and even – dare I say – more than the sacramental gifts. Indeed, the Church is called to be 'the universal sacrament of salvation', as Pope Paul VI says in *Lumen gentium*. This means, among other things, that the Church is to be a place where the faithful can grow in the faith, which includes growing in virtue.

To teach well we have to provide good conditions for learning, and what this looks like differs from context to context. It is well within the realm of possibility that some among us are suffering from health and mental health problems, or financial difficulties and precarious living situations, or troubled social and familial circumstances. If so, it is incumbent upon those who of us who have been tasked with teaching to offer practical help and support. Perhaps it is unusual to think of financial aid and advice as relevant to catechesis: but of course, other centres of learning are well aware that it is, and offer bursaries and scholarships to those who need them. Nor do we think of provisions for childcare in the context of catechesis, but on this point too, we can learn from other educational institutions. It might be objected that the Church is not a school: but of course, it is.

Having said earlier that I do not want to burden the clergy with yet more duties, I cannot offer the same comfort to the Church more broadly. There is much work to do before we can claim to take the task of catechesis seriously. It would be a mistake to think of this work as being supplementary: it just is the work of the Church, called as she is to raise disciples to be sent into the world.

Notes

1 Peter Garnsey and Anthony Bowen (trans. and eds), 2003, *Lactantius: Divine Institutes*, Liverpool: Liverpool University Press.

8

Instruction, Delight and Persuasion: Catechesis as Rhetoric

MARK CLAVIER

Catechesis is typically described in terms of an intellectual or informative process – the means whereby people are taught the essentials of the faith – that takes place within some formal framework of teaching: Sunday school or confirmation class. This chapter will argue, however, that catechesis is fundamentally a rhetorical activity, that the church is fundamentally a rhetorical community, and that the aim of catechesis is not just to convey the faith (*fides quae*) but also to foster the kind of imaginations that can receive and sustain that faith meaningfully. Without the fertile soil of the imagination, Christians will find their faith incomprehensible or absurd and ultimately uninspiring. The reason for this is that we never catechize in a neutral space. Those who are being instructed are already part of one or more communities that exert rhetorical force on how they understand the world, themselves and the happy life they choose to pursue. A successful catechesis must, therefore, begin by challenging the rhetoric of these communities. In short, the task of catechizing involves the heart as much as the mind.

Rhetorical Communities[1]

Rhetoric is 'the art of using language effectively so as to persuade or influence others'.[2] The aim of rhetoric is to gain consent to certain propositions or to convince people to undertake particular actions. As traditionally understood, rhetoric engages the emotions (pathos) in order to persuade less through rational discourse than by pleasure and delight. As articulated by Cicero, the goal of rhetoric is to 'present, please and persuade'[3] or 'through speech, to have hold [of] people's minds, to win over their inclinations, to drive them at will in one direction, to draw them at will from another'.[4] Typically, rhetoric has been considered a public function, a way of engaging effectively and purposively with groups of people: an audience, a crowd, a courtroom, deliberative body, the republic.

While Roman rhetoricians such as Cicero and Quintilian placed rhetorical agency within a particular set of people (orators), the term 'rhetorical community' recognizes that the basis of rhetoric is the community itself. As articulated by writers such as Charles Taylor and James K. A. Smith, the social imaginary and discourse contain rhetoric force – our belonging to others and sharing a common discourse disposes us to embrace or reject some beliefs, undertake or refuse some actions, and conceive or ignore some kinds of self-conception.[5] The shared Latin root of communication, community and communion indicates the centrality of discourse to common identities and perceptions.[6] The social discourse of rhetorical communities influences how its members perceive and reflect upon their individual and collective experience and defines the happy life they pursue. In this way, rhetorical communities invoke the reality its members take as obvious and axiomatic.

Consumerism as a Rhetorical Community

Consumerism functions as a rhetorical community that establishes a conception of the happy life, shapes self and collective identity, and disposes people to embrace one range of beliefs over others. In many ways, describing consumerism as a rhetorical community should be uncontroversial. Most citizens of western countries live within a society suffused with messages: television, films, advertising, the Internet, magazines, popular songs, and so on. Moreover, a great many of these messages (by one estimate an average of 10,000 per day) are deliberately rhetorical, seeking to persuade their audience to part with their money. Within consumer societies, marketing and advertising are the most pervasive forms of rhetoric. According to Stuart Ewen, advertising is the 'prevailing social language' of consumer societies.[7] Consumers now live perpetually in or only a click away from the marketplace.

Modern-day marketing has its roots in the social psychology of the early twentieth century.[8] Drawing on the insights of Sigmund Freud, early social psychologists sought to understand the mind of what they call 'crowd'. Particularly influential in America was the writer and political commentator Walter Lippmann, whose *Public Opinion* argued that people rely on 'mediums of fiction' to organize data into coherent narratives. Lippmann writes:

> By fictions I do not mean lies. I mean a representation of the environment which is in lesser or greater degree made by man himself ... A work of fiction may have almost any degree of fidelity, and so long as the degree of fidelity can be taken into account, fiction is not misleading. In fact, human culture is very largely the selection, the rearrangement, the tracing of patterns upon, and the stylizing of, what William James called 'the random irradiations and resettlements of our ideas.' The alternative to the use of fictions is direct exposure to the ebb and flow of sensation. That is not a real alternative ... For the real environment is altogether too big, too complex, and too fleeting for direct acquaintance. We are not equipped to deal with so much subtlety, so much variety, so many permutations and combinations. And although we have to act in that environment, we have to reconstruct it on a simpler model before we can manage with it. To traverse the world men must have maps of the world.[9]

Lippmann argued further that as modern life grows more complex, people's perception of reality necessarily relies increasingly on external authorities: that is, what they learned through the media or from acceptable authorities. Though he did not express his ideas in these terms, Lippmann was effectively arguing for a rhetorical understanding of reality. Much of what people believe about the world is what they have been persuaded to believe.

After World War Two, public relations specialists (then a profession in its infancy) drew on Lippmann's insight to devise lifestyle marketing strategies for American businesses. These presented images of the ideal or happy life rather than technical information about products. By associating their commodities with idyllic portrayals of happiness, marketers persuaded people to pursue happiness by purchasing their advertised products. For example, one of the first marketing campaigns created an emotional attachment between the 'open road' and freedom and democracy (in the face of Soviet threat) in order to sell cars.[10] With the development of radio, television, computing and the Internet, the reach and pervasiveness of lifestyle marketing expanded exponentially. From the cradle to the grave, people's lives today are filled with professionally designed presentations of the happy life that deliberately attempt to influence how they perceive themselves and their world.

Although marketed ideals of happiness and fulfilment may individually differ, almost all share two basic assumptions: first, that the happy life is achievable in the here and now and, second, that it is best pursued through the consumption of products and services. The sociologist Zygmunt Bauman notes, 'The society of consumers is perhaps the only society in human history to promise happiness in earthly life, happiness here and now, and in every successive "now"; in short, an instant and perpetual happiness.'[11] What facilitates the pursuit of happiness within consumerism is the free market, which maximizes freedom of choice. This is the fundamental message of consumer society – if you will, its gospel – which is received primarily at the emotional, precognitive level. In short, lifestyle marketing works because we are fundamentally people who reach out into the world less with our minds than with our hearts.

Consumerism functions rhetorically on three levels. Globally, it demarcates the rhetorical community that promotes the idea that happiness is pursued through mass consumption; that is the market's overarching rhetoric, sustained by the oratory of millions of marketers. Next, consumerism's rhetoric functions tribally in the form of identity groups based on shared patterns of consumption (e.g. football fans, gamers, runners, Goths). These fluid 'consumer tribes' generate the lifestyles and social niches within consumerism that give individuals a sense of belonging. Such tribes employ goods and services not only to express themselves collectively but also to attract new membership. Finally, the rhetoric of consumerism functions individually in the way people understand and present themselves. People want not only to be cool, but also to be seen to be cool. Individual consumers become walking billboards, presenting themselves in ways they believe express themselves or will make an impact on others. Self-expression is essentially a form of advertising.

The net effect of these different levels of rhetoric is to invoke an encompassing social imaginary from which a range of beliefs emerge or are discarded. Consumerism's 'medium of fiction' articulates a reality that encourages certain social practices, discourses and ideas (e.g. individualism, valorization of choice, expectations about happiness, high levels of consumption, waste, weakening social capital, and perhaps a bias towards growing inequalities). That reality also makes some beliefs and activities central to the Christian faith incomprehensible or anathema as can be seen not only in the various controversies within the Church but also in the collapse of Sunday worship attendance and the authority of the Church and its hierarchy. This is not to pass judgement on any of these things but only to note that it is no coincidence that they should be controverted or rejected mainly in consumer cultures.

Increasingly, churches have felt compelled to conform to the rhetoric of consumerism and to align their own beliefs and practices accordingly. As Martyn Percy notes:

Increased mobility, globalization, and consumerism have infected and affected the churches, just as they have touched every other aspect of social life. Duty is dead; the customer is king. It is no surprise, therefore, to discover churches adopting a consumerist mentality and competing with one another for souls, members, or entering the marketplace itself and trying to convert tired customers into revitalized Christians.[12]

It is perhaps no coincidence that this same period has witnessed a general collapse in various forms of catechesis (especially Sunday school and confirmation classes) – too many consumers, even Christian ones, are not convinced of the relevance of the Church's teaching to their daily lives.

Catechizing Consumers

We are now in a position to see why catechesis is often ineffective. Churches typically make two mistakes in their approach to catechism. The first is to take no account of the rhetorical forces at play by treating people as essentially rational individuals in need of only formal instruction in the faith. This approach prioritizes the matter of faith (*fides quae*) by teaching basic doctrine and practice; it informs people's minds without engaging their hearts and thus does not challenge the rhetoric that is shaping their understanding of reality. James K. A. Smith argues that this 'reduces the Christian faith primarily to a set of ideas, principles, claims and propositions that are known and believed'.[13] While the Church instructs people about what they ought to believe and perhaps how they ought to live, consumer culture continues to encourage them to embrace other ways of living and believing through emotional appeal and the promise of this-worldly happiness.

The other approach, popular among evangelicals, accounts for our social and cultural context in terms of competing worldviews. For example, in *Living at the Crossroads: An Introduction to Christian Worldview*, Michael Goheen argues,

Christian mission ... requires the development of a Christian worldview ... If we refuse to develop and indwell a Christian worldview, we will merely leave ourselves vulnerable to the

influence of the worldviews present in the culture that sur-
rounds us. But if we are serious about bearing witness to the
Lord Christ with the integrity and depth that such witness
requires in our modern day, the development and appro-
priation of a Christian worldview rooted in the drama of
Scripture will become a priority. Our mission demands it.[14]

While this approach tries to articulate the different layers of
people's social and cultural commitments, it fails to consider
the rhetorical power of worldviews. People do not subscribe to
a worldview because they have chosen it rationally from a list
of possibilities. Nor can they typically switch from one worldview to another by simply having it described and assessed. It
is not a matter of being taught a 'biblical worldview' and then
embracing it. Individuals are disposed towards a consumer
worldview not by rational argument but through a long and
relentless exposure to its rhetoric that continues during and
after their instruction in the faith.[15] This rhetoric also disposes
them to accept or reject various religious commitments on
offer.

If formal instruction in doctrine or an articulation of a
so-called Christian worldview are not effective forms of catechesis, what then is? Catechesis needs to begin by recognizing
that its aim is to draw people from one rhetorical community to
another. In the early Church, the catechetical process, involving lengthy instruction, prayer, and even exorcism, facilitated a
conversion not only to Christianity but also away from pagan-
ism. The catechetical process involved a movement away from
a pagan social discourse towards a Christian one, including the
amendment of social and individual habits. This is why, for
example, Christians were warned away from public spectacles
(like the theatre and arena) and struggled with the appropri-
ateness of reading profane literature. Rhetorically understood,
catechism was a form of instruction that brought individuals
from one rhetorical community (the world) into another (the
Church).

But such catechesis must go beyond only formal instruction. In Book Four of *On Christian Teaching*, Augustine draws

broadly on his own training as a rhetorician and more pre-
cisely on Cicero to describe the aim of Christian teaching: 'to
instruct, delight, and move their listeners'.[16] In the background
of Augustine's approach is the classical distinction between
wisdom and eloquence – philosophy and rhetoric – that Cicero
had tried in his own treatises to unite by arguing that eloquence
is the means whereby people can receive wisdom. Augustine
explains, 'A hearer must be delighted so that he can be gripped
and made to listen, and moved so that he can be impelled to
action.'[17] Eloquence persuades people to embrace doctrine.[18]

Eloquence or delight plays a threefold role within his scheme.
First, it attracts attention; Augustine makes the obvious point
that it is futile to teach if no one listens. Second, it maintains
attention so that the audience does not become distracted,
especially by the rhetoric of other teachers. Finally, it makes
the wisdom more palatable and agreeable so that the audience,
swayed by its delight in the instructor's eloquence, wants to
accept and believe what it is taught. What persuades listeners
is not the truth itself (except when the truth in and of itself
delights) but the eloquent presentation of that truth. Augustine
earlier explains:

> Eloquent speakers give pleasure, wise ones salvation ... We
> often have to take bitter medicines, and we must always
> avoid sweet things that are dangerous: but what better than
> sweet things that give health, or medicines that are sweet?
> The more we are attracted by sweetness, the easier it is for
> medicine to do its healing work.[19]

A spoonful of sugar helps the doctrinal medicine to go down.
Catechesis, therefore, needs to undertake the process of instruction in a way that instructs, delights and persuades. People
need to be encouraged to want to believe what the Church is
teaching them.

Towards a Catechetical Community

How might this be done? The obvious answer would seemingly be to make catechesis more entertaining. Entertainment has been shown to be an easy and effective way to attract and hold attention; rhetorically it is incredibly powerful as evidenced by its ubiquity in marketing. Entertainment can also be an effective vehicle for spreading information and inculcating values. For this reason, arguably the primary approach to catechesis in a broad range of churches for the past 50-plus years has been to make heavy use of amusing activities: films, games, field trips, and the like. But there are two problems with relying too heavily on entertainment.

First, it arguably cedes too much ground to the prevailing consumer culture, seeking to out-perform consumerism in its own form of rhetoric. The Church is rarely able to stimulate and amuse as professionally or effectively as shopping malls and the film/music/gaming industry nor does it have the expertise, analysis and funding available to marketers and entertainers. Mark Yaconelli describes this approach as 'ministries of distraction' that respond to anxieties of teen angst and congregational anxieties by 'providing virtual environments with virtual relationships that keep youth distracted from the deeper rhythms and practices of the Christian faith'.[20] Yaconelli points out that this approach tends to be expensive and ineffective in engendering a commitment to faith that outlasts adolescence. Recent surveys of church attendance in the States seem to support his conclusion.[21]

Second, while entertainment tends to be self-oriented, delight requires love. 'We only love what delights us' wrote Augustine, a sentiment echoed later and widely in medieval theology.[22] According to Bonaventure, delight is the pleasure that arises in the soul when it encounters beauty, sweetness, or wholesomeness – the 'invisible attributes of God' – that ultimately draw the understanding towards God.[23] A similar sentiment is expressed in the seventeenth century by Richard Baxter:

Nothing is more easily confessed by all, than the desirable-
ness of delight and pleasure; and the most excellent object,
which must be most beloved, must be our chief delight; for
love itself is a delighting act, unless some stop do turn it aside
into fears and sorrow. Nothing can itself be so delectable
as God, the chief Good; and no enjoyment so delectable as
loving him.[24]

For Augustine and much of the western tradition, delight is
fundamentally the presence of the Holy Spirit, conceived as the
shared delight of the Father and the Son.[25]
A theological link between delight and the Holy Spirit takes
us back to the idea of a rhetorical community. If the Holy
Spirit is associated with God's delight, then its source is the
love shared within the Trinity and by the Trinity with the faithful. Augustine explains:

So by what is common to them [love], both the Father and
Son wished us to have communion both with them and
among ourselves; by this gift, which they both possess as one,
they wished to gather us together and make us one, that is to
say, by the Holy Spirit who is God and gift of God. By this
gift we are reconciled to the godhead, and are delighted by
love, and it enables us both to know things more thoroughly
and to enjoy them when known more happily.[26]

Thus, delight is found within the community of the church
in the love shared among its members, including those being
catechized. Without that shared love (*koinonia*), churches
are forced to rely on alternative – one might say, artificial –
sources of delight that are not wedded in any obvious way to
the theology being taught.
Instructing, delighting and persuading, therefore, are the
task of the whole rhetorical community of the church. Specific
courses of instruction are set within catechetical communities
where the guiding principle for everything – be it worship,
teaching, pastoral care, or service to the community – is both
instruction and delight. In marketing parlance, churches

remain 'on message', conveying the symbols, stories and teachings of the Church through their various activities. But they also seek to engage in their ministries and mission in ways that inspire and delight, thereby touching people's affections (for each other, their ministers and their church), which then disposes them to receive what their community believes and to find their ultimate delight in God.

This is where the catholic liturgical tradition has a rich treasury. During Advent, for example, congregations light candles, sing Advent hymns such as 'O Come, O Come Emmanuel', and enjoy seasonal treats like mince pies and mulled wine. These activities and customs sit alongside the liturgy and inspire a certain affection for the Advent season and receive the main themes of that season. From this perspective, despite the oft-bemoaned commercialization of Christmas, that holiday's popularity and the increased attendance at services demonstrate what happens when the Church manages to connect instruction with delight. Invocations of the 'meaning of Christmas' may fall far short of robust theological accounts of the incarnation, but they do demonstrate popular attempts to express and encourage Christian teaching expressed by the nativity. The Catholic tradition contains similar examples throughout the year that speak to people's hearts and by doing so inform their imaginations and connect their affections to the narrative of the Church and especially Christ's ministry. This then fosters a stronger sense of belonging to the Church as a distinct community and greater receptivity to its liturgical cycle of instruction.

Finally, however, there needs to be a recognition that the Church's instruction and delight are continually challenged by the rhetoric of consumerism. There is no real escape from the world's rhetorical community. Christians are caught in two competing worlds, torn by the rhetoric of each. Moreover, those availing themselves of catechism are not themselves unformed but have very likely spent their life as consumers, perhaps even uncritically so. Thus, they (like all Christians) must be aided in their discernment of and appreciation for God's delight.

Catechesis must seek to disrupt the rhetoric of consumerism

by articulating its own rhetoric: the basic narrative of Scripture and the Church. As Hauerwas argues, for the world to know that it is the world, the Church needs to 'enable the world to strike hard against something which is an alternative to what the world offers'.[27] But then catechesis must develop what Augustine calls the 'palate of the heart' that allows people to taste the delight that is God.[28] This happens through the experience of prayer, worship, mutual love, and in how the Church engages with its own narrative and presents that narrative in ways that delight and inspire. If the Church is a story-formed community (to use Stanley Hauerwas's description), then it needs to learn to tell its story eloquently.

The Church must also rediscover the *beati vita*, a distinctly Christian notion of the happy life. As has been seen, consumer culture and marketers articulate a very clear and appealing ideal of the happy life. It is on display not only in the various lifestyle marketing campaigns discussed earlier but also in the lives of the rich and famous: the saints of consumerism. Catechesis must have at its heart an equally robust vision of the happy life and the eloquence to present it in a way that excites people. Surely there are contemporary equivalents to the saints of old whose lives model Christian beatitude and whose stories excite the imagination.[29] But ultimately, unless glimpses of happiness can be found within the actual and visible community of the Church, articulations of the happy life will not convince. This once more takes us back to the need for *koinonia*, for a unique experience of mutual love and delight within worshipping communities.

A catechetical church needs to be persuasive church. There is no point in teaching if we cannot persuade people to embrace the Christian faith. But no instruction can be truly persuasive unless it is eloquent, inspiring people with its message and encouraging them to delight in God. Our goal is not just to teach the biblical narrative but also to nurture a delight in it; not just to teach people how to worship but also to nurture a delight in it; not just to foster the twofold command of love but also to nurture a delight in both God and our neighbour. None of these goals can be achieved except by belonging to a community in which its very life instructs, delights and persuades people towards these goals. That requires a discourse and inner life characterized by enacted love and fellowship. That is ultimately the work of the Holy Spirit, poured out into the hearts of the faithful whom he fuses together into the Body of Christ. That same Holy Spirit is also the basis of our rhetoric: the gospel, which to teach should be our chief delight.

Notes

1 For a full discussion of rhetorical communities, consumerism and the Church, see Mark Clavier, 2019, *On Consumer Culture, Identity, the Church and the Rhetorics of Delight*, New York: Bloomsbury.

2 *Oxford English Dictionary Online*, 2016.

3 Cicero, *Orator* 69.

4 Cicero, *The Ideal Orator* 1.30.

5 See Charles Taylor, 1992, *Sources of the Self: The Making of the Modern Identity*, Cambridge: Harvard University Press; and James K. A. Smith, 2013, *Imagining the Kingdom: How Worship Works*, Grand Rapids: Baker Academic.

6 Oliver O'Donovan, 2002, *Common Objects of Love: Moral Reflection and the Shaping of Morality: The 2001 Stob Lectures*, Grand Rapids: William B. Eerdmans, pp. 26–7.

7 Stuart Ewen, 1988, *All Consuming Images: The Politics of Style*, New York: Basic Books, p. xvi.

8 For further reading on the development of public relations, see Stuart Ewen, 1996, *PR!: A Social History*, New York: Basic Books.

9 Walter Lippmann, 1998, *Public Opinion*, New Brunswick: Transaction Publishers, p. 16.

10 Edward Bernays, 1947, 'The Engineering of Consent', *The Annals of the American Academy of Political and Social Science* 250, pp. 113–20.

11 Zygmunt Bauman, 2007, *Consuming Life*, Cambridge: Polity Press, p. 44.

12 Martyn Percy, 2005, *Engaging with Contemporary Culture: Christianity, Theology, and the Concrete Church*, Aldershot: Ashgate, p. 65.

13 James K. A. Smith, 2009, *Desiring the Kingdom: Worship, Worldview, and Cultural Formation*, Grand Rapids: Baker Academic, p. 33.

14 Michael Goheen, 2008, *Living at the Crossroads: An Introduction to Christian Worldview*, London: SPCK, p. 29.

15 Smith, *Desiring the Kingdom*, pp. 32–3.

16 Augustine, *On Christian Teaching* 4.12.27.

17 Augustine, *On Christian Teaching* 4.12.27.

18 For a more detailed discussion of this, see Mark Clavier, 2014, *Eloquent Wisdom: Rhetoric, Cosmology, and Delight in Augustine of Hippo*, Turnhout: Brepols, pp. 70–85.

19 Augustine, *On Christian Teaching* 4.5.8.

20 Mark Yaconelli, 2006, *Contemplative Youth Ministry: Practising the Presence of Jesus with Young People*, London: SPCK, p. 24.

21 See, for example, Pew Research Center's Religion and Public Life Project, 2015, 'America's Changing Religious Landscape', which indicates a veritable collapse in religious affiliation among young American adults.

22 Augustine, *Sermon* 150.3, 'On the connection between love and delight in medieval theology', see Clavier, *Eloquent Wisdom*, pp. 253–73.

23 Bonaventure, *The Soul's Journey into God* 2.5–13 (referencing Rom. 1.20).

24 Richard Baxter, 1830, *The Reasons of the Christian Faith*, 8.11.41.

25 See, for example, Augustine, *On the Trinity* 6.11-12.

26 Augustine, *Sermon* 71.18.

27 Stanley Hauerwas and William H. Willimon, 1989, *Resident Aliens: Life in the Christian Colony*, Nashville: Abingdon Press, p. 94.

28 Franz Posset, 2001, 'The "Palate of the Heart" in Augustine and Medieval Spirituality', in Frederick Van Fleteren and Joseph C. Schnaubet, OSA (eds), 2004, *Augustine: Biblical Exegete*, New York: Peter Lang, pp. 253–69.

29 A worthwhile catechetical project in this regard would be the retelling of saints' lives in a modern register that reformulates earlier hagiographies according to contemporary tastes.

9

'Let the Little Children Come to Me': Catechesis of Children

CLARE GARDOM

'What does God look like?'

My first feeling on hearing the question was alarm. I felt caught out, as if the child had found a loose thread that threatened to unravel the whole of Children's Church. Next came resentment: we were just tidying up to go back to 'big church' and it was an inconvenient time for an unanswerable question.

A different adult replied patiently and encouragingly: 'Not like anything. You can't see God.' The child was not satisfied. 'So God's invisible: doesn't God exist then?' 'Well, God isn't a thing like other things. Maybe God is more like a verb, a "doing word".' The child didn't look altogether convinced by this mysterious explanation, but she didn't seem to think she had asked a silly question, nor been given a silly answer.

If I'd had to give an answer, I think it would have been similar to the one given, but my nervousness would probably have communicated itself, indicating that this sort of questioning was dangerous and unwelcome. My inner reaction reflects my own Sunday school formation. I grew up in Zimbabwe, where a more conservative church and educational system aimed to give children a simple, confident faith backed up with extensive knowledge of Bible verses. In that context, asking a question indicated a lack of knowledge or understanding, which would be remedied by a knowledgeable adult quoting (and if necessary, explaining) a passage of Scripture. If the question could not be answered like this, then it was the wrong sort of question to be asking.

In this chapter I want to explore how catechesis of children might develop beyond the model familiar from my youth. This is necessary for two main reasons. First, as Mark Clavier argues in Chapter 8, catechesis does not take place in a vacuum. Educational methods have rightly evolved to encourage independent thought, enquiry and dialogue: a child who is used to this at school will expect nothing less at church. Faith needs to be shown to be capacious enough to accommodate lively minds. Otherwise those minds will conclude that faith is only for people who prefer to think narrowly and do not question. The next generation of theologians will be lost.

There is a more fundamental reason why this model is unsatisfactory. God is invisible. Not just beyond our sight but beyond all our senses, unknowable and indescribable. Everything we have to say about God is partial and imperfect, from a child's first faltering attempts to understand 'who Jesus' daddy is' to the most nuanced description of the Trinity. Because of this, neither simple nor complex answers to children's questions about God will ever provide the final word. One response to this is silence: if we can't say anything true about God then we should say nothing. This is called the apophatic approach and is not commonly taken by catechists.

A lot of what children learn about God doesn't come through our words, though. Children are constantly absorbing information through all their senses. For this reason, a more formal liturgical setting can be accessible to a young child in a way that a service with less ritual is not. Music, bells, incense, candlelight reflected in the chalice all communicate something of the divine. Children learn the rhythms of the church year tangibly: an Advent calendar or Jesse tree at home, an Advent wreath at church, slightly simpler food in Lent, exciting after-church biscuits, communicate more than lengthy explanations. An Orthodox icon is an excellent focal point for prayers at church or home. We have one of the Holy Family: our baby kisses them sloppily, like he kisses us. He is learning, physically, to participate in our shared faith.

If we are going to plough on with our inadequate words, we can at least admit their inadequacy to children. Children are used to not knowing things; their worlds are full of uncharted territory. Baptized babies are already full members of the body of Christ, which shows just how little having all the answers has got to do with it. 'Beloved, we are God's children now; what we will be has not yet been revealed. What we do know is this: when he is revealed, we will be like him, for we will see him as he is' (1 John 3.2). Catechesis is what happens now, before 'what we will be' has been revealed, and before we see God as God is. We, the children of God, are beginning to grow up, but it is not a process that will be completed in this life. This is the case for all ages: catechizing literal children is essentially the same as catechizing adults; the differences are stylistic rather than theological. God is still catechizing you and may use the children in front of you in that process, just as God is using you to catechize them.

How does God catechize us? Through Jesus Christ (the answer's always 'Jesus' at Sunday school). Clement of Alexandria styles Christ as 'educator' (*paidagogos*), a figure in classical education who was responsible not just for imparting information, but for bringing children up in the right habits of mind and behaviour: 'Let us call Him, then, by the one title: Educator of little ones, an Educator who does not simply follow behind, but who leads the way, for His aim is to improve the soul, not just to instruct it; to guide to a life of virtue, not merely to one of knowledge.'[1] The best nursery and primary-school teachers embody this aim, and those responsible for children's catechesis at church should aspire to it, too. Clement goes on to describe the virtuous habits appropriate to a propertied Christian man in the second-century Roman Empire, quoting Scripture to support his views. When discussing table manners, for example, he cites Romans 14.20: 'Do not, for the sake of food, destroy the work of God', and 1 Corinthians 10.31: 'So, whether you eat or drink, or whatever you do, do everything for the glory of God.' He takes these texts to mean:

We must keep ourselves free of any suspicion of boorishness or of intemperance, by partaking of what is set before us politely, keeping our hands, as well as our chin and our couch, clean, and by preserving proper decorum of conduct, without twisting about or acting unmannerly while we are swallowing our food. Rather, we should put our hand out only in turn, from time to time; keep from speaking while eating, for speech is inarticulate and ill-mannered when the mouth is full, and the tongue, impeded by the food, cannot function properly but utters only indistinct sounds.[2]

While Clement's uncompromising stance on talking with one's mouth full may endear him to harassed parents, overall the details of his advice are not especially transferable. But I think his text contains a crucial insight that really is useful for children and their catechists.

Clement's detailed prescriptions for food, drink, dress and behaviour make the fundamental point that Christ is present in our small daily actions. This is a great resource in making sense of children's catechesis, since children and those who care for them spend most of their time engaged in daily, practical, often tedious habits. A very small proportion of their time is spent in church, or engaged in powerful or heroic activities. We can easily start to think that the Christian life is being lived elsewhere, probably by people without children, who are able to devote themselves to prayer and study without distraction. In fact, the Christian life is being lived, well or badly, wherever Christians are living. The incarnation infuses all human action with divine significance. The Holy Family presumably spent most of their time on those small, tedious actions: making a mess and tidying up, again and again and again. (Did Mary ever wonder if she could have served God better if she hadn't become a mother?) Feeding the hungry, giving a drink to the thirsty, clothing the naked, are literally what caring for a small child involves. Can we believe we are doing these things for Christ, as he claims we are in Matthew 25.40? How would we do them, if we did believe it? And yet 'Christ has no body now but yours', as the saying attributed to St Teresa of Avila goes

– Christ in the carer, Christ in the cared-for. The simplest stuff of daily life is a participation in the ever-flowing love of God.

Adults should be very careful not to abuse this insight by theologizing their own preferences for children's behaviour (some of Clement's prescriptions, such as the table manners text quoted earlier, contain more than a hint of this). A good way of checking is by imagining having the law that we are laying down quoted back at us by a child unhappy with our own behaviour. Would we feel affronted or convicted? While the incarnation brings God among us, it does not solve the mystery of God; the cloud of unknowing is impenetrable even to parents. On the question, 'Does God care if I eat my broccoli?' we are agnostic. Nevertheless, all parts of the physical world, even the piles of damp laundry or overdue library books, are the potential arena for God's love and grace. We catechize children partly by recognizing and articulating this and behaving accordingly.

**

So, we have a model for our catechesis in the person of Christ, and some sense of the risks involved in hijacking the figure of Christ to back up our own agenda. How, then, did Christ teach his disciples? Principally through stories: the same stories that form the backbone of our catechesis of adults and children. Stories are part of the cataphatic alternative to silence in the face of our inability to describe God. The 'cataphatic' or affirmative way involves using everything at our disposal – art, music, theology, interpretive dance – to try and describe God. Like a child's picture of someone he loves, they are not perfect representations, but we make them anyway and offer God the whole big painty, glittery pile. They are maps of the half-known, with sea monsters and distorted coastlines, but their uncertainty honours our ignorance where clear lines of apparent accuracy would be arrogant fiction.

Throughout Christian history, people have looked for ways to tame the parables, to tie them down to one specific interpretation. Mark claims that Jesus gave the disciples explanations in private (Mark 4.34). Yet the stories remain multifaceted, revealing different insights on rereading: our sympathies or even our sense of 'what it's really about' can change radically. Some stories seem to be the same story over again: the lost sheep, the lost son, the lost coin. Some seemed incomprehensible to Jesus' original listeners (Mark 4.13). I find some incomprehensible now. What are we to do with these stories? We use stories to understand the world. The stories we were told as children sink into us, forgotten but forming us like our earliest food. Images, phrases and plots are stored away as interpretive tools for future use, or used to make sense of memories for which we did not previously have words. In *Reading and Loving*, her book on childhood literacy, Leila Berg writes of the excitement a small child feels on recognizing a picture of ducks in a book:

> That child was putting into those pictures all the remembered reality of feeding real ducks on a pond – the noise, the splashing, the flapping, the snatching – the duck who grabs everything, and the duck who gets nothing – and that, for him, was what these pictures were to which he was responding with so much glee.[3]

Berg herself thinks the pictures unsatisfactory and unlifelike: 'crude, pointless, jumbled', but considers that the child's delight at recognizing the remembered experience enables him to bridge the gap between the picture and reality. Even a preverbal one-year-old can feel 'the true excitement that comes to someone who has experienced something for the very first time, and is having that emotionally and physically delighting experience evoked again by the pages of a book'.[4]

We use stories to understand ourselves. When we read picture books to a small child, we instinctively 'put the child in' the story: 'which cake would you like?' we ask, and the child 'takes' the cake she likes best. For this to work, some aspects of the story need to be recognizable to the child. Arguing for the need for more diverse children's books, Berg suggested that the working-class children of 1960s London had no incentive to learn to read, since the books they had did not reflect their lives: 'The majority of children who now read, cannot read about themselves ... they see no recognition, no reflection of themselves, nothing that tells them they belong in this world; they grow up feeling they have no right to exist.'[5] Why learn to read if you don't see yourself in the story? Berg wrote a series of school reading books called 'Nippers', where the characters' lives reflected those of the children she had met. When she read them to children in a London East End school, their delight and amusement astonished her:

> What I had heard was the astonishingly helplessly physical laughter of release from tension, the laughter of acceptance, of recognition. For the first time with a shock of delight those children ... had seen themselves portrayed in preserves that hitherto were middle-class and alien. They didn't have to pretend to be someone else anymore. They were released. Not only did this release and acceptance in the classrooms – this startled joyful recognition of phrases and situations – turn books into friends, and make the whole business of learning to read affectionate. But in the relation it produces – because you're there, you're known, you're accepted – is the beginning of growth, spreading out. I've never forgotten that day.[6]

The release that comes from being known and accepted frees you for growth. If you think the Christian faith is worth sharing with children, it is because you have felt this release, this being known, within it. You have found your deepest sense of recognition within it and think that others may find this too. Without this, going to church is just an arcane hobby, and catechizing children an exercise in passing on a depreciating form of social capital.

Look at the language Berg uses to describe these children's sense of recognition: released, known, accepted, startled, joyful. St Augustine said something similar about reading the passage of Scripture that precipitated his conversion: 'I neither wanted nor needed to read further. Immediately, the end of the sentence was like a light of sanctuary poured into my heart; every shadow of doubt melted away.'[7] Romans 13, the passage Augustine is referring to, is not exactly a story, but it gave Augustine that same sense: that 'people whom we've never known, who live in centuries past, magically know us, and put us in a book'.[8] In turn, Augustine offers his own story to future readers, to see if they too feel that thrill of recognition. In his recent book on Augustine, James K. A. Smith likens the *Confessions* to narratives of addiction shared by members of Alcoholics Anonymous. The point of such narratives is not originality, he explains, but 'witness authority': the opportunity for others to recognize themselves in your story. He writes: 'To find ourselves in someone's story is not unique to addicts, surely. Rather, the brokenness of addiction only distils what is a human hunger: to be known, to find a place, to be given a story that gives us bearings, a sense of identity that comes from solidarity.'[9] In telling his own story, Smith argues, Augustine is inviting readers to recognize their own lives: 'What the *Confessions* ask of a reader is not, "What do you think of Augustine?" but rather, "Who do you think you are?"'[10]

Catechesis is an invitation into the story of salvation. We do it because in this story we have found ourselves known, accepted, released. We do it by sharing many stories: the ones Jesus told his followers; the ones they told about him; the ones that Jesus himself had heard and was formed by, in which he recognized himself ('today this scripture has been fulfilled in your hearing', Luke 4.21); and all the ones, like Augustine's, by people who found themselves known and freed and shared their stories in turn. When we offer children these stories, we need to do so in ways that communicate the rich freedom that they offer. It is all too tempting to present them deboned and pre-prepared for easy consumption with the moral nicely spelled out at the end. We do this because that's how we were taught as children, by people who thought we would not understand the story, or would wilfully misinterpret it out of wickedness or stupidity. Thus, we teach children (as we were taught), that there is only one possible correct interpretation, which the grown-ups know and you don't, so you'd better listen carefully or you'll get it wrong. At the same time, we are teaching them that Christianity is a combination of the blindingly obvious ('be nice to people') and the utterly puzzling (Jesus cursing the fig tree in Matthew 21) which you're not supposed to ask about. This is a faith that all God's children need to grow out of.

How can we avoid this? Go back to the stories. Trust their power, and the intelligence of the children. Like the little boy with the shoddy duck book, children are generous in bridging imaginative gaps with their excitement, if we let them. Give children the space and time to inhabit the story and make it their own. Prioritize the telling, acting and discussing of a Bible reading or saint's life. Let it be a real, open discussion: don't use it as an excuse to test the children. It's best if everyone acts the story out together: that way you are really playing rather than performing. It is the embodied, physical version of an Ignatian imaginative contemplation (a way of imagining oneself into a passage of Scripture, inspired by St Ignatius Loyola).[11] If the adults let themselves join in seriously, they may find it surprisingly moving. Not much is needed in the way of props, though any piece of cloth will probably find a use. What matters most is the atmosphere, which needs to be one of serious play. Nobody can play if they're worried about making mistakes, so correction should be as gentle as possible and avoided unless really necessary. Older children might start to feel uncomfortable: see whether they'll join in in the spirit of 'helping the little ones'. If not, perhaps they are ready for a more internal Ignatian contemplation of the story.

Children will only want to read the Christian story if they can recognize themselves in it. The words we often associate with children – small, simple, dependent – are an adult's view. Each child is the biggest and most complicated person she's ever been. By playing in the stories, children can be free for a moment from their own and others' narratives about them – the timid child playing reckless St Peter; goody-two-shoes as Herod. They are allowed to sympathize with characters whom a tidied-up version would have closed down to them: who hasn't felt some sympathy with the prodigal son's brother? They can try out different parts and find that all the parts of themselves are known and embraced by God. Younger children are unselfconscious about playing the part of Jesus, in a way that adults are often embarrassed to do. Why should we be? Didn't he give 'power to become children of God' to all who receive him (John 1.12)? Woe to any adult who projects this embarrassment by teasing a child eager to play Jesus: 'occasions for stumbling are bound to come, but woe to the one by whom the stumbling block comes!' (Matt. 18.7).

Good catechesis is particular to the people involved. There are many ways it can be accomplished in a church setting, and different levels of resources in churches will have an effect on how it can be done. At my church the children's Sunday catechesis is very simple, and while other contexts might find other ways of faithful catechesis, ours is I think an effective example of the use of story.

The children's worship at our church is structured around stories and ritual. Families arrive gradually and sit down on cushions arranged in a circle. There is a simple liturgy following the structure of a Eucharist: newcomers can follow the laminated sheets, which babies especially love to chew. If there are any new people or people who haven't been for a while we go round the circle and introduce ourselves. We sing lots: the opening prayer, the closing blessing, the song that introduces the 'feast' of bread and grapes. Non-verbal children can begin to recognize the structure of the session by the different songs. After a simple confession a singing slot, where children make requests. There is a shared repertoire, with words in a folder, which are offered to visitors. Some are action songs, some involve dancing in a circle or jumping up and down while singing antiphonally. When I first went, pining for 'real' church and reeling at the way becoming a parent had interrupted my prayer life, I was disconcerted by the sight of so many highly intelligent adults skipping round the room in their socks. Now it doesn't seem any weirder to me than the more sedate liturgical conventions across the road at 'big church'.

Next comes the story. Someone reads from the children's Bible – there is a rota and one family has prepared to lead in advance. A discussion follows, introduced by the people who are leading that week, but with frequent interruptions and interventions on all sides. It is both chaotic and collaborative: parents engage with other people's children as well as their own. There is a range of levels of familiarity with church and theological experience: it's not unusual to hear an adult exclaim 'I never knew that!' Then comes an activity based on the reading: either acting or craft. Then the children help to prepare and hand round the feast of bread and grapes. Then we sing our closing song, and go back to big church.

If we've timed it right, we get there just in time to go up for communion first, before the adult congregation. Then we sit at the back keeping reasonably quiet, out of sight but with a great view of the sanctuary because of the wide aisle. There are beanbags, books and quiet toys for us. During the final hymn we gather at the front of the south aisle by a statue of Mary and baby Jesus to sing the Angelus: a responsorial prayer, drawn from the text of Luke 1, commemorating the annunciation and incarnation. It is said and sung in Roman Catholic and Anglo-Catholic churches. The priest leads the Angelus, often holding their own or somebody else's child. Some children climb into the pulpit. Babies are passed round so older toddlers get a turn to be held up. The whole congregation is reminded that Jesus was a baby; these children are his children, and so are we.

* * *

Once I was looking at a prayer card with my daughter before putting her to bed: she was almost three. The card had a quotation from Psalm 23 and picture of two lambs lying in some grass. I told her that we were like the lambs and God was our shepherd who looked after us. We found a series of pictures in her story Bible of Jesus the good shepherd looking for the lost sheep, finding it and carrying it home on his shoulders. She moved ever so slightly, and I could see from her face that she was the sheep. In our little bleaty voices we thanked the shepherd for keeping us safe from wolves, for rescuing us and feeding us. It was the least wriggly bedtime prayers we'd had in a while, and I congratulated myself on my excellent catechesis. As I said goodnight, she turned to me and whispered, 'let's be pigs next!'

I can't remember whether we did play 'Jesus the good pigherd' the following evening, whether images of the Gadarene swine prevented me, or we just forgot. But I was struck by the skill with which she took on the story. She knew that God loves and cares for his creatures, fleecy sheep, porky piglets, and girls who are almost three. She knew this because by inhabiting the story and being the sheep she had recognized herself in it – its feelings of lostness and aloneness and joy at being found by the shepherd. She knew that a little lost pig would feel the same, and so would a lost girl, a lost child, a lost child of God.

We invite the children whom we catechize into these stories in the hope that they will recognize themselves. We hope that they take them on as their own to grow and live into, and that in a future that we will not see, they will find our maps still serviceable in charting the ever mysterious love of God.

Notes

1 Simon P. Wood (trans.), 2008, *Clement of Alexandria: Christ the Educator*, Fathers of the Church Patristic Series, Washington DC: Catholic University of America Press, p. 4.

2 Clement of Alexandria, *Christ the Educator*, Washington DC: Catholic University of America Press, 1954, p. 104.

3 Leila Berg, 1977, *Reading and Loving*, London: Routledge and Kegan Paul, p. 25.

4 Berg, 1977, p. 25.

5 Berg, 1977, p. 23f.

6 Berg, 1977, p. 88.

7 Carolyn J-B. Hammond (trans.), 2014, *Augustine: Confessions I*, Loeb Classical Library, Cambridge, MA: Harvard University Press, p. 411.

8 Berg, 1977, p. 74.

9 James K. A. Smith, 2019, *On the Road with Saint Augustine: A Real World Spirituality for Restless Hearts*, Grand Rapids, MI: Brazos Press, p. 159.

10 Smith, 2019, p. 161.

11 See Timothy M. Gallagher, 2008, *An Ignatian Introduction to Prayer: Scriptural Reflections According to the Spiritual Exercises*, New York: Crossroad Publishing Company.

Conclusion

JARRED MERCER

> Let knowledge, then, be used as a certain scaffolding by which the building of love may arise to remain for eternity, even when knowledge is destroyed. Used for the purpose of love, knowledge is highly beneficial, but of itself without such an end, it is proven to be not only superfluous, but also dangerous.
> (Augustine of Hippo, *Letter* 55, 21.39)

From various angles and perspectives this book has argued consistently that Christian formation and teaching, what we call catechesis, is a holistic enterprise involving the whole person. It is not just about right thinking but right and holy living. From beginnings in prayer and worship, to the formal teaching of doctrine and preaching, to the framing of the imagination and the bringing up of children, catechesis is communal, transformative and *lived*. We cannot pretend our task is complete by running a theology course or Bible study, or by holding confirmation classes or teaching Sunday school. These are vital, maybe essential, practices, but being a part of forming others in faith is ultimately training in the art of living. To be precise, it is training in the art of living in the way of Jesus.

Christians believe that Christ is the fullness of humanity, so that this way of life is actually what is most natural and normative for us, but it certainly goes against the grain of the life we know and the world we live in. The life to which we are called is a life of endless, senseless love in a world that is continually drawing lines and borders that love refuses to cross. The love of Christ, this love we are called to 'echo', blows the borders of our love wide open, but our lifetime is a school in which we learn what that love means and how we can join it. What this book has proposed throughout is that the community of the Church is the classroom.

All of the activities and practices of the community's life are instructive and transformative – they teach us and they shape and renew us. Scripture gives us a language of how to speak about God, a grammar of how to know God – it is wisdom and understanding. But more than that, God shows up in its pages – we find ourselves in dialogue with who God is and discover who we really are in turn. The liturgy and worship of the Church involves an opening up to knowledge of the God we are worshipping. The prayers, the words we say together, the creeds we confess reveal the God who loves us. But more than that, our worship shapes us towards that love as, most directly in the sacrament, we offer our whole selves to God and receive ourselves back anew and transformed. In the mission of the Church, we follow Christ's instructions to serve those in need, to proclaim the good news, to bring justice to an unjust world. In addition, as we serve we begin to see those we serve with the very eyes of Christ and, indeed, even meet Christ in them: 'Whatever you did to the least of these who are members of my family you did it to me' (Matt. 25.40).

And when we think about the direct action of teaching and formal catechesis, St Augustine said it well: 'Let knowledge, then, be used as a certain scaffolding by which the building of love may arise to remain for eternity.' In teaching we are doing nothing more and nothing less than seeking to build up and support love. Catechesis is as much an act of pastoral care as grief counselling, or spiritual direction, or anything else, because at each step we must with great sensitivity and affection seek to touch and turn the heart.

This involves our own approach to faith, our demeanour in teaching, our patience and ability to listen and learn ourselves, and our commitment to never compartmentalize Christian teaching from the reality of our everyday life – including the hard questions we cannot answer and the darkness in ourselves and our world that we would rather forget.

Being a catechist also, of course, involves the more obvious component of being a learned person. For some this sounds intimidating. But I'm not saying that the catechist has to be a world-leading scholar, I am only saying that they have to be committed to the renewal of their mind – which involves being a continual student of Scripture, theology *and* our world in a way that strengthens our affection for God and our neighbours. It means we are prayerfully working towards living with wisdom and discernment in all things, not just gaining knowledge about one thing. Because that yields a knowledge that is real and beneficial, a knowledge that builds love.

Index of Bible References

Index of Names and Subjects